# BUTTON PUSHER

# BUTTON PUSHER

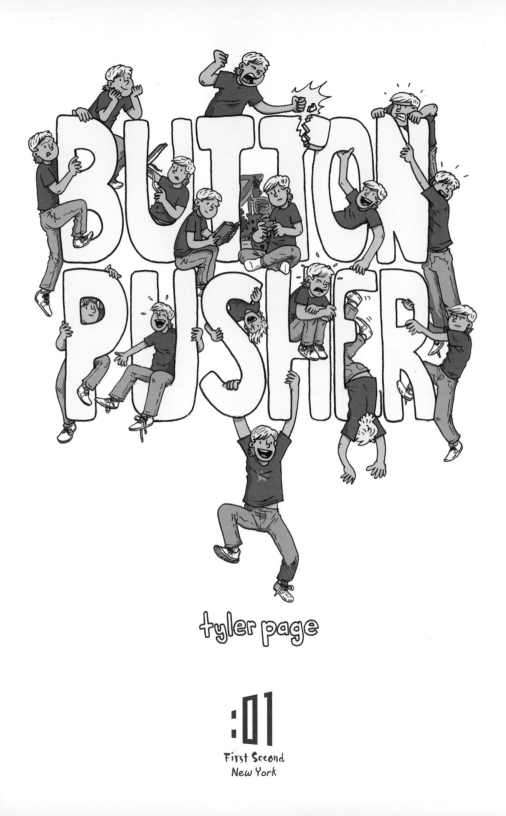

tyler page

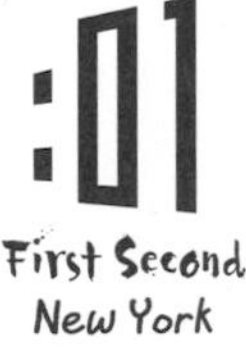

First Second
New York

TYLER!

Hurry up or you'll miss the bus!

Don't forget to turn in your permission slip!
Okay!
NURSE
Twins
Great Starts

I've got that presentation to the city planning commission today...
C'mon.
Finish this last bite, then we have to get you off to day care.
Great Starts
BILL

...so I might be late getting home.
NDY 50
I suppose I can take the kids to my drawing class if I have to.

Have a good day!
SMOOCH

Bye, Mom!
Don't forget your binder!

MAAAAA-UUUHHHM! It's a **TRAPPER KEEPER!**

Have a good day at school!

Hey!
My sister gave me all her Lisa Frank folders!
Cool!

Hey,
Dan!
Hey,
Tyler!
Morning!
Hi,
Pete!
I got a new
Ninja Turtle for
my birthday.
Turins
ESPRIT

I finished that drawing you
wanted, Nate!
RUMMAGE
RUMMAGE

Oh WOW!
Cool!

Ooh!
This is
awesome!
Whoa,
I love the
dragon wings!

And the claws are so sweet!
EWW! Gross!
ESPIRIT

You're just jealous you can't draw like that!
Pffft!

BUS!
This is an awesome drawing—thanks!
Sure—it was fun to do!

Tyler's, like, the best drawer in our grade!
Yeah!
195

Do you have any more cool drawings?
No—but...

Check out...
THIS!
Oh WOW—it looks so old!
My grandpa gave it to me. It was his from World War II!

Ooh—this seat is so soft and rubbery!
That's crazy!
I can't believe he let you have it!

I wonder...

Whoa—
WHAT?!
SSSLICE
It was like scratching an itch.

WHAT ARE YOU DOING, KID?!

I don't know what the heck you were thinking, kid—off to the principal's office!
I didn't even think about it.

PRINCIPAL

All right, young man.
Do you want to tell me why on earth you cut up a bus seat?!

WELL?!
Uh... I don't know.
I really didn't.

Maybe you were trying to prove you were tough?
NO
I...
I just wondered what it would be like to cut the seat and did it.

I just...
I wondered...
There must be **SOME** reason, young man.
Property damage is a serious crime!

We can sit here all morning. You need to tell me why you did this. And where did you get the knife?
Well, my grandpa—

PRINCIPAL

I **KNEW** we shouldn't have let you have that knife. I am **SO** embarrassed!

What would possess you to **DO** something like that?!
WHY?!
SIGH
Wait until your father hears about this...

This is the second time I've been called this month!
We have to do something about your behavior.

Can I still watch Transformers?
No. Go to your room until dinner.

I initially made this appointment because he's been having a lot of headaches lately.
Group Health Bloomington Clinic

But then the thing on the bus happened and...
I don't know. He's always been such a handful...

After talking to the social worker, it really sounds like they want him to see a counselor.

Tell me about your home life—what are your family dynamics like?
I—
SNRT

SOB
SOB
SOB

OH it's a mess!
SNIFF
We've been married ten years, and I'm on the verge of calling it quits...

Their father is a good provider, but he has a very bad temper. He...he...
Has he hurt you or the children?

No—No, nothing like that...

He yells.
WHEATIES

He swears.
GOD DAMN #!@$ PIECE OF $#!@

He smashes things.

He spanks the children.
SMAK
SMAK
WAH

I was SNIFF raised in a Quaker church and don't believe in spanking, but he does...
LATEX EX

You never know what will set him off!

And the children see all of this?

Yes. SOB Sometimes.
I'm sorry!
SOB
Well...

Often, the family environment can contribute to a child's behavior, so it's a good idea to get a sense of that.
SNRT

I think family counseling might be a good place to start.

Oh, their father won't go along with that.
It really sounds like the school will want some counseling. I think a family setting would be a good first step.

Tell your husband it's what the school wants, that it's in his son's best interest.
I can try. He might go along with that.

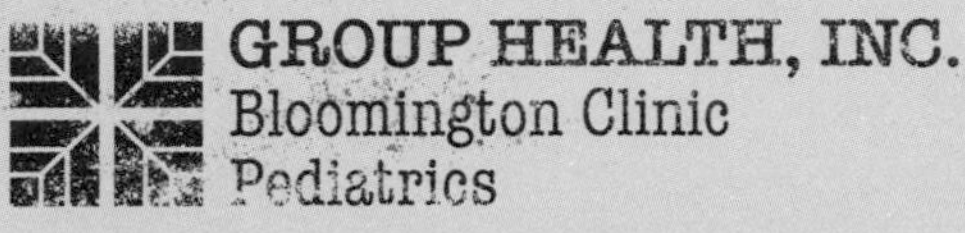


PATIENT INFO
3434 70 34
PAGE, TYLER M
12 07 76

PATIENT VISIT SUMMARY

Describe according to SOAP
-SUBJECTIVE
-OBJECTIVE
-ASSESSMENT
-PLAN

S: Tyler's been having headaches off and on for a couple months. Started when he got back to school. They're frontal or occipital; can make him nauseous and vomit.

He got in trouble at school taking a knife on the bus, cutting up some property. He didn't threaten anyone but the social worker said he seemed to have some repressed anger and wondered about the home situation. As it turns out, his father is a very perfectionist type A person who doesn't have a lot of time for the family. The children tend to hold their feelings in. Tyler's younger brother has a very flat affect most of the time. The father takes out anger on the mother. The school social worker felt that counseling might be necessary but the mother felt the father would not be open to this.

A: Tensions in the family. Disruptive school behavior.

P: Called mother back on phone to discuss: consider family counseling, the school will force it if he gets in more trouble. Tyler was flitting around from thing to thing during entire meeting. Family dynamics need to be explored more.

Problem: TENSIONS IN THE FAMILY. DISRUPTIVE SCHOOL BEHAVIOR.

Signature:

Owen Rogers, M.D./tag

GROUP HEALTH PROGRESS NOTES PLAN, INC.

Okay—let's go over the answers for these problems I've put on the board.
ARMATAGE ELEMENTARY
The next answer is?
Seven!
Yes, seven. Good job!
Okay, and the next problem was seven minus three and

There's a big bug over by the wind—
TYLER?

Let's pay attention, please?
Okay—on to the next problem...
MATH

TYLER?

OH!
Sorry!

And the next one was eleven minus four...

TAP
TAP
TAP
TYLER?

**PLEASE?!** I'm not going to ask you again!

?

And that's it!
Let's see how everyone did.

Gosh—I didn't get **any** right. What did I do?

And how about you, Tyler?
Uh... I, uh, got them all wrong...

What happened here?
It looks like you added them all!

We've been talking about subtraction all morning.
That's what we were doing up on the board.

What have you been doing?
OH
I guess I didn't notice?

This became a pattern during my early school years.
Tyler—please! It's time to stay in our seats!
sharpening pencil for fifth time

It's not visiting time, Tyler. Please stop interrupting Nathan and do your worksheet.
BLAH BLAH BLAH

Tyler, you're supposed to be doing your reading work now.
CLAY

Stuff like that was always happening.
Ahem...
MATH
Uh...

It wasn't that I didn't like school but that I often had my own ideas about how to spend my time.
Tyler—I'm in the middle of a story!

And because of that, I often didn't finish my work on time.
You have to stay in from recess and finish your work.

Thank you for coming in, Mrs. Page.
Hi.
It's so nice to meet you!
BALL STATE

This is Ms. Sloan—the school social worker.
Nice to meet you.
And you too!

I know Tyler can be... difficult, but I know he's smart!

It's okay, Mrs. Page.
Tyler is a very bright boy. Very creative, but...
BALL STATE

Tyler is very...**challenging** to have in the classroom. He's constantly out of his seat. All over the classroom.
READ
It's like he's off in his own little world.

I thought he might settle down as the year progressed.
But it really hasn't gotten any better.
Oh.

And in light of what happened on the bus the other day, we really feel Tyler might benefit from some counseling.

That's what his doctor said.
Yes, I had the pleasure of talking to him yesterday, and I think he had a good idea.

About the family counseling?
Right, it would be a good way to ease into something like that so Tyler doesn't feel singled out.

I agree.
I can tell Tyler is a good kid.
But this is the kind of thing that could get out of control if we don't address it now.
Um-hmm.
Okay.
BALL STATE

Later.
12
BUTLER

12
BUTLER

This is good. You use the charcoal with such sensitivity.
Oh!
Thank you!

You should really think about signing up for the advanced class next semester.
If it works with my schedule, I will.

Cu-pid draw your
bow-ow and let
your arr-ow go-oh

I'm home!
Thanks for watching the kids!
Uh-huh.
TRIBUNE
Coming into turn five Unser Jr.— only twenty laps to go!

Did you all eat?
That was a close one!

Yeah, the kids had mac and cheese.

Did you get enough to eat?
Yeah.
BALL STATE

But I had to help Dad with the instructions.
sigh

Why don't you go play in the family room. I need to talk to Dad...

How was your class?
It was good. The teacher liked my work.
TRIBUNE
BALL STATE

I, uh... I met with Tyler's teacher this afternoon.

The school social worker and principal are insisting he see a counselor...
TRIBUNE
BALL STATE

And...

Dr. Rogers suggested family counseling would be a good start.
TRIBUNE
To make it easier for Tyler.

CRINKLE
CRINKLE

SNAP
Fine.
TRIBUNE

And so.
Thank you all for coming—it's nice to meet you!

Tyler, why don't you start by telling me how you've been feeling lately.

Suddenly my dad started crying.

It was such a weird situation.

I'm sorry!

I don't mean to get so upset. It just happens. I'm sorry!
I want to make sure...to make sure you know I love you guys.

I...I know Dad.

The two of you should really consider marriage counseling, to work out your own problems...

And I think Tyler would benefit from a group setting, with other kids his age.

SILENCE

The family counseling sessions continued.
It makes me scared when Dad throws things.

But they usually just ended up with my parents fighting.

Did you get in trouble for cutting the bus seat?
Kind of...
NINTENDO POWER

You have to use the ladder so you can cross the river.
Ah, cool!

Uh, they took the knife, talked to my parents. I had to talk to my doctor and some other people I guess.
TAP TAP
And then kill those guys!

SLASH
SLASH
BA-DINK
SLASH
DUH NUH NUH

Why **did** you cut the seat?

I dunno. I just wanted to see what it felt like, I guess.
Hm—
**OH**—wait— **here!** Go back to that other room!

Ah, sweet. I got it!
Boys?

Would you like a little popcorn for a snack?
Yeah!
Sure.

POP POP POP POP POP
POP POP POP POP POP

Here we go!
What's that?
It's microwave popcorn!
TEST PRODUCT NOT FOR SALE
My dad's working on it at his job.

Oh dang—it's the boss!
Hey, guys!
Ooh—how's the popcorn?
It's good, Dad.
I think you finally got it right!

Hey, honey—how was your day?
Not bad!
Yeah—you got it!

GET IT GET IT!
NO—with the bombs!
TAP TAP TAP TAP

ALL RIIIGHT!

Dinner's almost ready—we're having chicken.
Can Tyler stay?
Of course!

After that dungeon you have to go get the blue tunic.
Okay—cool!
Dinner's ready!

And here's the salad.

This is delicious, honey. Thanks for making dinner.
You're welcome.
Yeah—this is great!

Let us give thanks for this meal...
?

So did you boys have a good day at school?
Do Nate's parents ever fight like mine?

Where are we going again?
It's called group counseling.

It will be fun. You'll play games with other kids your age.
Why?

Well, you know how we've been doing counseling as a family?
Yeah.

This is just for you. You can be with kids your own age and...
PARKING
Group Health
Behavioral
Health

...maybe talk about anything that's bothering you or whatever.
You'll have fun!

Tyler, my name is Ron. I'll be leading your group.
KIDS GROUP 4:30P
Hi.
Why don't you run inside and find something to play with while we wait to start.

He'll be fine. We'll see you in about an hour, okay?
Okay.

I want to make sure you all understand you're not here because you've done something so bad...
...but because we want to help you understand **why** you do the things you do.

For instance, let's say... Stacy, maybe someone is mean to you at school. Picks on you. Calls you names.
Then you come home and hit your little brother for no reason.

Does that sound familiar?
Yeah...
NOD
NOD
NOD

Meanwhile my parents started marriage counseling.
I work sixty to seventy hours a week! She only works part-time!
He throws things and yells!
He breaks things!
He doesn't help with the kids or the housework!!
It was only the beginning of many years of therapy—as a family, solo, or at marriage retreats and workshops.
FIX YOUR MARRIAGE
HOW TO FIX YOUR MARRIAGE
At my group, we played games together...
Give everybody a chance!
Me! Me!
Over here!
...and talked about our feelings and what was happening in our lives.
FIDGET FIDGET FIDGET
I accidentally spilled a pot of boiling water on myself.
I'm ashamed of how I look.
My parents got divorced.
Now I never get to see my dad.
My mom died last year, and I'm never happy.
Uh... I do things without thinking about it?
I don't belong here. These other kids seem to have such serious problems...

I managed to make it through the school year.
I know Tyler has been a little challenging this year.
He has, but...
...I understand how difficult it can be when you're both working and you've got this little one, too.
ROOM 110

So I want to stress that while his behavior has been challenging, he is doing well academically.
PROGRESS REPORT
Oh, thank you!

He is very bright and creative. I think he just needs to mature a little more.
We appreciate your patience!

Good job, kiddo!

Who wants **ice cream?!**

With the arrival of summer, everyone's cares seemed to fade away.
Batter up!

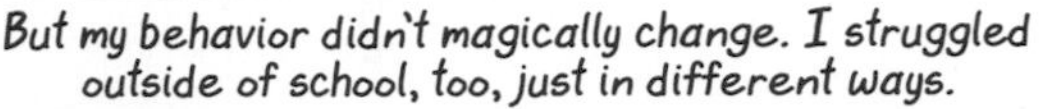
But my behavior didn't magically change. I struggled outside of school, too, just in different ways.

Okay, two ghosts on!
NOD

THROW
HIT

GOT IT!

You're out! HAHAHAHA
Aw man!

Ha ha, you're out! **You. Are. OUT.**
Wah wah!

OUT! OUT! OUT!
HA HA HA HA HA

Yeah, I was out, so what? C'mon, we've still got two more!
Ooh out!

Here...
**NOPE!**

**I've** got the ball—you'll never get it back!

?
Wacky Taco

♪Neener neener nee-**ner** ♫
Come on!
You're ruining the game!

You'll never get me!

Can't get it!
**My ball!**
SLIP

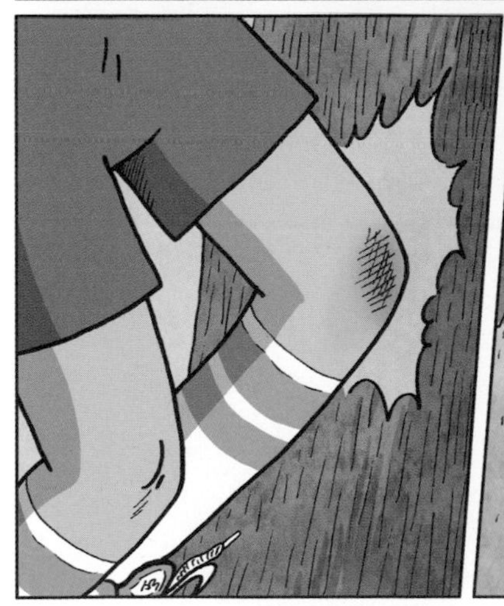

AAUGH!

What's wrong with you?!

Yeah, why do you always have to be such a **weirdo?!**
You always take things too far!

Why ***did*** I do that?
I was just trying to have fun, be silly.
And then it was like a switch flipped and I wasn't in control of myself.

NO

BUT:

In the simplest terms, my brain was—**IS**—different than most people's.

The parts of my brain responsible for...

PLANNING

IMPULSE CONTROL

SHORT-TERM MEMORY

REWARD

TASK MANAGEMENT

MOTIVATION

FOCUS

SHORT-TERM MEMORY

CROSS-TEMPORAL ASSOCIATION

*Huh?! We'll define this later!*

*were developing more slowly than usual and also having difficulty communicating with other parts of my brain.*

These are sometimes called

# "EXECUTIVE FUNCTIONS"

*because they are the tools our brains use to* **CONTROL OURSELVES AND OUR IMPULSES.**

When we're babies, we simply react to our environments. But as we age, these parts of our brains develop to help us act with intent.

Our brain uses these tools to...

filter distractions

prioritize tasks

set and achieve goals

control impulses

...among other things.

Without executive functions, it would be like if there were no traffic signs or signals on our roads—your thoughts would go racing all over the place!

It can definitely be disruptive and cause problems when you have a hard time controlling yourself.

– BUT –
some people think this is why many ADHDers are such intuitive learners and creative problem solvers.

Our brains are wide-open highways with surging rivers of ideas and thoughts, and occasionally interesting suggestions or ideas result.

Maybe that's why I spent a lot of time playing by myself. There was no one to tell me what I could or couldn't do. I made up my own little worlds.
SNAP

OH NO—we're going to crash!

Hurry, get the truck out of the way!

KER-ASH!

YELL SCREAM
CRASH

SWEAR YELL SHOUT
Wah!

CRASH YELL SHOUT
What happened?
I don't know.
Dad... yelling...

They're fighting again, aren't they?
It's okay.

We'll be stuck up here all night!
Good thing we already had dinner, I guess.

SWEARYELLSCREAM
Garfield

SWEAR CRASH YELL BREAK SCREAM YELL SHOUT
This is what all families are like, right?

Things didn't change much for me when school started again.
BRIIIIIIIIIIIIIIING
Recess!

Tyler?

You can't go out to recess today. You need to finish your work from this morning, remember?
Oh yeah.

I found it easy to focus and work in the quiet.

DONE!

Bring it up here. Let me see.

Mm-hmm, yes, yes, correct...

Very good...but recess time is just finishing.
BLUE PLANET
Oh...

**Try harder** tomorrow to get your work done on time.

Did you see how far I jumped?!
What kind of bug was that?
Oh yuck!
GUESS
17
Think I stepped in something gross...

I have to run a quick errand, so I'm just dropping you off.
But I'll be back before you're done.
Group Healt
Behavioral
Health
Okay.

MIT

Huh.

I've never seen a fire alarm like that.

The plastic is so smooth.
I wonder how it works...

Ooh—the spring is **so** strong!

BBBBRRIIIIIIIIIIIIIIIIIIINNG

EVERYONE OUT QUICKLY!
GET ACROSS—
MIT

AHEM

False alarm, everyone—false alarm!

You're going to talk to the firefighters when they get here...
EE-OOH WEE-OOH
MIT
Okay...

Soon.

Ah, Mrs. Page, just the person I wanted to talk to.
**Oh no!** What happened?!

Right after you dropped Tyler off, he pulled a fire alarm!
Oh gosh! I'm **so** sorry!

It's... It's okay. He **claims** he was just touching it when it went off...
Well, he **is** very curious about things, but...

Honestly, this is just a bigger manifestation of the behavior I wanted to talk to you about anyway.

The more we see of Tyler, the more apparent his...**active** nature is. It's quite, well, hyperactive.

He has real trouble calming down once he's excited.
He can't sit still.
And he's constantly doing impulsive things. Even here.

He seems unable to tell us exactly why he does the things he does. He tells us they "just happen."
What can we do?

His doctor hoped a setting like this might help him, but I don't feel like it's making much of a difference.

I don't think his problems are just social or psychological.

It might be time to start thinking about other options.

All right, the next word is "shirt."
READ
sharpen
Sharpen
Sharpen

whisper whisper
Heh heh!

See how I gave him fangs in this one?
ATCH

Did you see DuckTales yesterday?
Shh!

That's a cool pencil!
Tyler? Please?

Tyler?
**Please!**
Stay in your seat!
Sharpen
Sharpen
Sharpen

Sorry!
And then the last word is "shadow."

Uh...

I missed some words...
You should have been paying attention.

It looks like you missed "shirt," "shallow," and "shadow."

Okay.
AND

Here is the worksheet you missed this morning. Why don't you take it home to finish?

TYLER!
...

Oh. Right. Sorry.

Later that afternoon.
Finish up that worksheet first and then you go out and play, okay?
Here's your milk.

Next on Donahue...

DONE!

I'm going over to Pete's!
Really? Okay...

How'd he finish this so fast...?
He got all the answers right, too...

OWIE

MOOOOOOM
SNOZZ
Z

What!
What is it?!
HE-MAN

My ear! OW! It hurts! **OWIE!**
Nnngghh—**c'mon!** I have to work in the morning!

Let's take a look.
OW

Does this hurt?
TUG TUG
AH!
OWIE! OWIE!

Probably another ear infection...
SOB

It's too late to go to urgent care...
I'm sorry, honey.

Let's start with some Tylenol...

...and we'll get the heating pad.

Here—lay your ear on the hot pad.That will help.

Shh... Shh... Shh...
Oww...

Shh... Shh...
STROKE STROKE

The moon shown through the window shade

Aaand the pixie man danced right through
The little man danced and he danced and he danced and he danced and he sang this song

It's eight o'clock
It's time to go to bed
It's eight o'clock
You little sleepy head
Shh...
Snzzz

Hm, yes.
It does look quite inflamed.

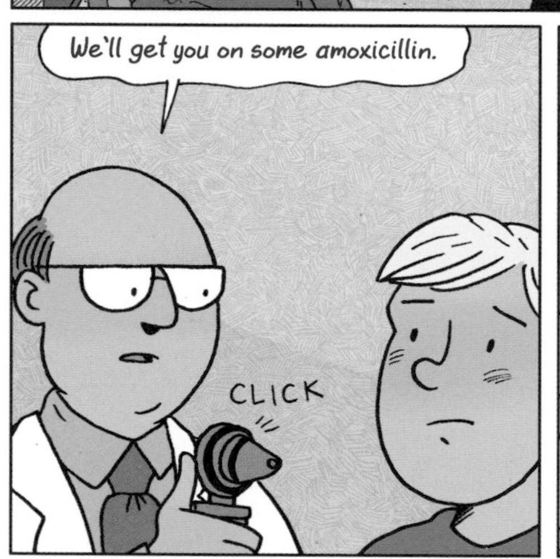
We'll get you on some amoxicillin.
CLICK

You can get down now, young man.
I'd like to chat with your mother.

We need to talk about his behavior.

It sounds like he's still having a lot of trouble at school?
Yes. And the other day his group counselor brought up the issue of hyperactivity.

Yes, we spoke on the phone this morning.

I think it's time for us to do a more thorough evaluation of his behavior.

My husband said I should ask about something called...uh...Ritalin?
Would that help him?

That is a possibility, yes.
But I'd like to do a little more observation first.

SHOVE

KNOCK KNOCK
Hello?

Ah, Mr. Page, thank you for coming in.
Hey, pal!

Oh, hey, Dad!

Tyler, why don't you take your brother out into the waiting area so I can talk to your mom and dad.
All right, c'mon.

Stay in the lobby, okay?

ELCHAIR
Based on what his teachers and group counselor have said, his behavior certainly isn't getting any better.

Is he getting enough sleep?
I think so...

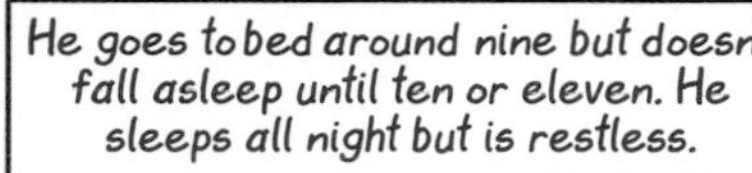
He goes to bed around nine but doesn't fall asleep until ten or eleven. He sleeps all night but is restless.

Yeah, he tears up the sheets, kicks them around.

Hm...

I've been hearing about this "attention deficit" thing—is that what this is?

# ADHD*

## ATTENTION DEFICIT HYPERACTIVITY DISORDER

*prior to 1987 it was Attention Deficit Disorder or ADD

ADHD is basically a pattern of inattention and/or hyperactive-impulsive behavior that

1. LASTS MORE THAN SIX MONTHS
2. OCCURS IN MORE THAN ONE ENVIRONMENT (HOME AND SCHOOL, ETC.)
3. INTERFERES WITH NORMAL FUNCTIONING OR DEVELOPMENT

It was once thought to be a form of brain damage but is now considered a ***neurodevelopmental disorder***, meaning



The ADHD label is what's called a

## CLINICAL DIAGNOSIS

There are no medical or laboratory tests involved. A clinical diagnosis is based on interviews, observation, and assessment by a medical professional.

Whereas a medical diagnosis such as diabetes involves laboratory tests such as measuring blood sugar and insulin levels, etc.

ADHD is not like the flu or heart disease or cancer.

This can't happen

It's not even one specific thing.

ADHD is really a label for a bunch of symptoms that commonly occur together.

Developmentally inappropriate levels of...

Inattention
Hyperactivity
Impulsivity
Emotional Control

which make it more difficult to interact with the world.

There is no one single **CAUSE** of ADHD.

It's best to think in terms of

COM PO NENTS

**MEANING**
many things can contribute to the symptoms people with ADHD ultimately express.

**GENETICS** is one of the strongest, or primary, components.

Your brain has developed the way it has in large part because of the genes passed on to you by your family.

The ADHD brain is physically "wired" differently than most people's.

And this is why, especially for children, there is such a hard time controlling behavior: Those mental tools for self-regulation and self-control are not at the same level as their peers' and aren't "hooked up" in the same way.

How did you eat all the cookies?
I couldn't control myself.

We've seen how that can end up causing problems or getting you in trouble because you end up doing things without thinking about them or considering the consequences.

What?!
You wrote your name with deoderant on the back of the door?
WHY?!
I don't know...
Tyler

research has shown that, at the end of the day, people with ADHD reach the same level of development as neurotypicals.

(It just takes a little longer for us to get there.)

# RESEARCH

has identified several "candidate" genes that are more frequently found in those of us with an ADHD diagnosis.

These genes have been observed to impair/interact with brain areas and pathways related to Executive Functions.

## Candidate Genes

- Serotonin HTR 1B Receptor
- Serotonin Transporter
- Synaptosomal-Associated Protein 25
- Dopamine Beta Hydroxylase
- Dopamine Transporter
- Dopamine D5 Receptor
- Dopamine D4 Receptor
- ADRA2A
- 5-HTT
- TPH2

These findings have helped with the notion of

**"DIMENSIONALITY"** in ADHD ➡ The concept that it's not the same for everyone and the challenges people with ADHD face vary from person to person.

How can he have ADD? He's been playing Legos for hours...

Such dimensionality may be a product of which genes are present.

If, for example, there are seven genes that predispose a person to ADHD, those genes might be active, absent, or present (but dormant) in various combinations. Those combinations affect the strength of the symptoms and behaviors a person expresses. This may be why we see a few primary "subtypes" of ADHD.

Primarily inattentive

Primarily hyperactive

There are also
ENVIRONMENTAL FACTORS

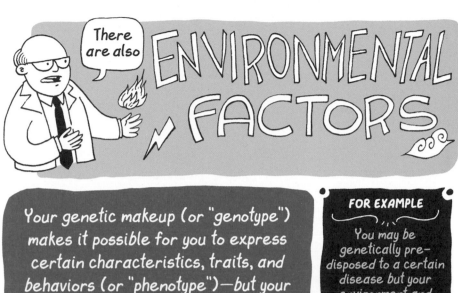

Your genetic makeup (or "genotype") makes it possible for you to express certain characteristics, traits, and behaviors (or "phenotype")—but your environment often dictates how or if you actually do manifest them.

**FOR EXAMPLE**

You may be genetically predisposed to a certain disease but your environment and experiences can dictate if you get sick or not.

Many life experiences and psychosocial factors can come into play.

- Things that happen to you in the womb (like a mother who smokes or physical trauma)
- Dysfunctional, harmful, or inadequate social relationships
- Stress or trauma
- Complications in pregnancy
- Ethnic background and culture
- Socioeconomic status (SES) (poor/rich, education, etc.)
- Diet
- Environmental toxins (smoke, lead, etc.)
- Access to health care
- ETC.

These are all things that can influence whether or not, and to what degree, a trait is expressed.

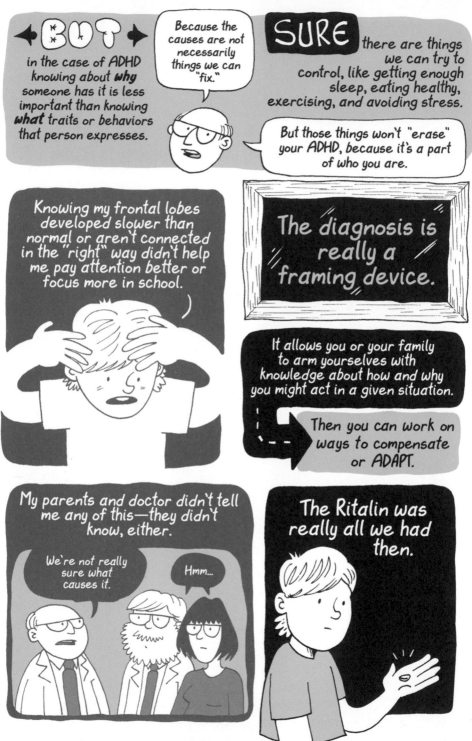

BUT

in the case of ADHD knowing about **why** someone has it is less important than knowing **what** traits or behaviors that person expresses.

Because the causes are not necessarily things we can "fix."

SURE there are things we can try to control, like getting enough sleep, eating healthy, exercising, and avoiding stress.

But those things won't "erase" your ADHD, because it's a part of who you are.

Knowing my frontal lobes developed slower than normal or aren't connected in the "right" way didn't help me pay attention better or focus more in school.

The diagnosis is really a framing device.

It allows you or your family to arm yourselves with knowledge about how and why you might act in a given situation.

Then you can work on ways to compensate or ADAPT.

My parents and doctor didn't tell me any of this—they didn't know, either.

The Ritalin was really all we had then.

Tell me—what were things like for you in school?
Fine, I suppose. I don't recall having any real problems.

I did well, but...
I did have some trouble paying attention.

I did okay kind of half paying attention until about sixth grade.
I remember things getting trickier then.
I would be bored with most stuff unless it was something that really interested me.

Even now I still have problems like that. If I have to work out a tricky math formula it takes me forever.
But the stuff that really interests me is a breeze.

Hm, well...
I think the next step is to do some formal testing and observation. That should give us an idea of how to move forward.

You mean like medication?

Yes. That could very well be a possibility.

Here's some information that should answer some of your questions.
Okay, we'll look it over.
WHAT IS ADD?
CIBA
Huh...

Hmm...

"It sounds like the father himself has some attention deficit, which has actually persisted into adult life."

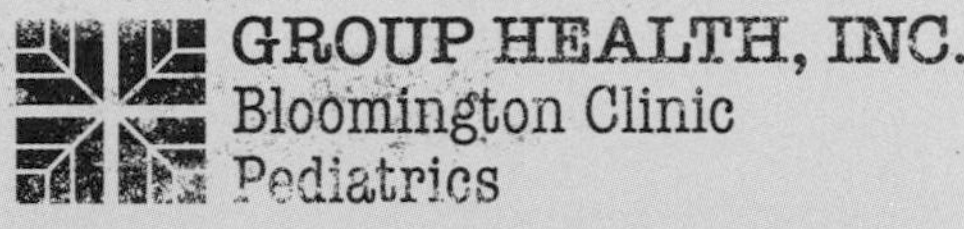

**GROUP HEALTH, INC.**
Bloomington Clinic
Pediatrics

**PATIENT INFO**
3434 70 34
PAGE, TYLER M
12 07 76

PATIENT VISIT SUMMARY

Describe according to SOAP
-SUBJECTIVE
-OBJECTIVE
-ASSESSMENT
-PLAN

S: Earache. Also questions about behavior. Tyler has had problems in school concentrating on his work and staying in his seat. This has been a problem basically since he started school. He talks to other kids, his attention wanders, and he often has to stay in from recess to finish work.

Tyler is in a group for kids w/ behavior problems. Questions of hyperactivity have been brought up. Parents want to discuss this more. He's also a restless sleeper, tears up the bed at night. Doesn't seem to snore.

When I talked to parents alone, the father says he had trouble concentrating in school and even has trouble now unless it's something he's really interested in. Still has trouble focusing as an adult.

O: Inflammation in ear.

A: Otitis media. Questionable hyperactive behavior, possible attention deficit. Large tonsils, might be disturbing sleep.

P: Amoxicillin for ten days for ear. We'll do a more thorough evaluation of his behavior. Parents are wondering about Ritalin.

Talked to parents alone about possible Ritalin for attention deficit. It sounds like the father himself has some attention deficit, which has actually persisted into adult life.

We need to be careful not to attack Tyler's self-image. His dissatisfaction w/ his performance in school is starting to affect it already. He's very bright and articulate.

Problem: OTITIS MEDIA. QUESTIONABLE HYPERACTIVE BEHAVIOR.

Signature:
Owen Rogers, M.D./tag

GROUP HEALTH PROGRESS NOTES PLAN, INC.

My mom said she left money so we could order pizza!
Sweet—we should get Domino's!
LARC
LARC
LARC
17
LARC
12

BEEP BOOP PEW PEW ZAP BEEP PEW PEW
LARC
12

DING DONG
OOH—
The pizza!

$12.75 out of twenty...
And here's your—
LARC

PIZZA MAN PIZZA MAN!!
LARC
LARC

PIZZA MAN!
YAY! PIZZA MAN!
LARC
LARC

Uh—here's your change.
Have a nice night...heh heh.
Thanks.
LARC

SLAM
UGH! What the heck were you **doing**?!
Heh heh.
LARC

God—that was **so** embarrassing!
SHOVE
HA HA HA HA He heh...
LARC

Whattaya mean? You should have **seen** your face—it was hilarious!
Jeez!
Why do you always have to be **such** a **weirdo**?
LARC
LARC

NOM NOM
NOM
NOM NOM

Do you wanna keep playing Contra?
Not really. What else could we do?

I know! Let's make a haunted house to scare my parents when they get home!
Ooh—yeah!

There should be a bunch of stuff down here we can use!

RUMMAGE
RUMMAGE

We could rig something up with this!
Actually... I've got an idea!

WHUT
is going on here?!
LARC
Uh...
LARC
Get your butts down here!
NOW!

Later.
You have to stop and **think** before you do things!
...weigh the consequences!

It's not just about not getting in trouble...
You could have gotten **hurt!**
LARC
What if you or Nate had fallen?!

What if you'd broken your leg?
Or your neck?!
LARC

We were just messing around. I didn't think about it.
Well you have to **try**.

I will.
LARC
You're grounded from Nate's for a week.

But I didn't try.
I couldn't.

Then the formal evaluations and observations began.
These questions are meant to be objective about your son's behavior.
So try to be as honest as you can.
Tyler!
Please? Sit down!
READ
That's the **sixth** time he's gotten up in the last **fifteen minutes!**
Do you feel you have a hard time paying attention in class when other things are going on?
Huh?
Oh.
Sometimes.
GOOSEBERRY
And how often would you say you have to redirect Tyler to his work?
Every day.
Many times.

ANOTHER KISS
ROAD + TRACK
THE THIRD KISS

I don't know what else to do.
Nothing seems to work.

What if he fails out of school?
He needs to be able to get a good job someday!

But...medication?
Is it right?
ROAD + TRACK

All I know is he needs real help and this seems like a place to start.
Hm.

Soon.
Tyler's scoring results are back, and he scored **very** highly.
Both in home and in school.

I think it might be time to seriously consider a trial of medication...
That's what we were thinking, too.

What do the pills do?
Will there be side effects?
Will they make him sick?
How long will he have to take it for?

Ritalin is a low-level stimulant that seems to help kids like Tyler to focus and better control themselves.

It might suppress his appetite a little, but most kids tolerate it very well.
Okay.
NOD
Should I tell them **my** doctor had **me** try Ritalin a few years ago?

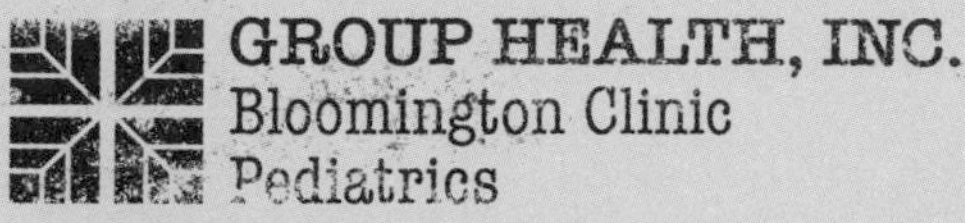


PATIENT INFO

3434 70 34

PAGE, TYLER M

12 07 76

PATIENT VISIT SUMMARY

Describe according to SOAP
-SUBJECTIVE
-OBJECTIVE
-ASSESSMENT
-PLAN

S: Behavior check. There has been no difference over the last week. His activity level doesn't seem to be affected by how much sleep he gets.

The scoring sheets are returned, and he scores very highly, both by his teachers and his parents.

They're all ready for a trial of medication. Parents had a lot of questions about the medication and side effects and I gave them the booklet by Larry B. Silver published by CIBA, Attention Deficit Disorders.

A: Attention Deficit Disorder.

P: Start w/ Ritalin 5mg in the morning as half of a 10. After 2 days go up to a whole 10mg tab in the morning. By the fifth day start on the 20mg SR in the morning. They should contact me in the next week or two about possibly adding 5 or 10mg in the afternoon. We'll plan to see him back after the holidays or they'll call if needed.

Problem: ATTENTION DEFICIT DISORDER. TRYING RITALIN.

Signature:

Owen Rogers, M.D./tag

GROUP HEALTH PROGRESS NOTES PLAN, INC.

A few days later.
Tyler, you know we've been talking about how you have a hard time controlling yourself.
Your impulses, what you focus on at school, staying in your seat, right?
Uh-huh.

And that's hard for you sometimes, isn't it?
I guess.

Sometimes it's okay to run around and be a little crazy, like at recess.
But other times you need to listen, and ask, and pay attention.

It's like...if you walked into a room and there was a big, red button, you might just walk over and **press it**...

And **then** ask what it does only to find out it launched a **nuclear missile**, eh?

So your mom and dad and your teachers and I have been talking. And you remember we did some tests?
We think we might be able to help you.

NOD
NOD

Honey, there's some medicine that might help you pay attention a little better at school, and we think you should try it.

You know how your mom might give you medicine for a head-ache? Well, this is a pill that should help you pay attention and not be so distracted, especially at school.

Okay.

I'll follow up with you in a few weeks to see how it's going.
Thank you!

Dear God, let this work.
I don't know what I'll do if it doesn't.
OPTICAL

The next day.
Now remember what we talked about?

You're going to take this every morning to see if it will help you pay attention a little better at school.
Uh-huh.

Good job. Now go brush your teeth before you miss the bus.
RUSTLE
RUSTLE

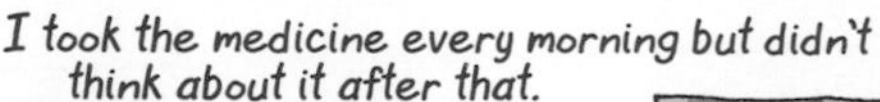
I took the medicine every morning but didn't think about it after that.

I didn't feel any different.

As far as I could tell, nothing changed.
Hey!
Did you see A-Team last night?!
Oh man!
Mr. T was **so** funny!

I went to school.

And played with my friends.

And soon...

TAP
Huh?

I said—did you figure out number seven yet?

Oh. Yeah. Sorry.
It's an adverb.
Thanks!

BBBRIIIIING

Tyler?

You finished all your work this morning, so you can go out to recess.
OH.

I made no conscious connection to the Ritalin.

A few weeks later.
And then Tyler climbed out the window onto the roof!
HA HA What?!
No way!

Yeah, he tied a rope to my dresser and just—
Whoa, scary!
It wasn't that scary!

Did you get in trouble?
Yeah—did you get grounded?

Nate's mom called my mom and—
He couldn't come over for a week!
My mom was **so** mad!

Who's ready for cake?

HAPPY BIRTHDAY TO YOOOOOOU

YAY!
YAY!

Oh wow, sweet!
I've got that guy! He's awesome!

Who wants ice cream with their cake?
ME! ME! ME! ME!

C'mon, Skeletor—you'll never get me!
Heh heh!

GET 'EM!
RING
RING

AARRGH!
Oh no—it's Beast Man! Look out!
THUMP
CRASH
BANG
Hello?
Oh yes, hi, Dr. Rogers!
He's actually having his birthday party right now.

He's been doing very well.
It's...kind of shocking how quickly it made a difference.
Look out! Here comes Trap Jaw!
RAARRGH!

I have noticed him having a harder time getting to sleep lately, but otherwise...
He seems fine!

Yes, I'll be sure to let you know if we notice anything else.
Can I have more cake, Mom?

Just a minute, honey. I'm on the phone.
Okay.

Oh? His father?
Um...

Not much has changed there. It's off and on. I never know what to expect with him...

He said he was going to try a different medication himself, so I guess we'll see.

Okay. Yes, of course. Thank you for checking in!

ALL RIGHT.
Who's ready to play some party games?!

DALE GARDEN
CENTER
NO.
It has to be a short-needle tree!
TRE

Well, what about this one?
It's too short!

How about these?
Oh those are cute. Sure!

This is the one.
Well? Give me a hand!

GRRRRRR

COME ON, YOU PIECE OF #@$& TREE!

You want **how** much?! It's a #$&@ tree!

GODDAMN SUNNUVVAAAH
DEN
TER

I don't understand why we can't get a long-needle tree one of these years...
Because I don't **like** long-needle trees. That's not what I had as a kid. Doesn't feel right.

We always had long-needle trees. They look so pretty. Maybe next year—
Just stop it, all right?! We're not getting a #!@& long-needle tree!

@#$!&

I said **pull!**
**PULL**

I said **left**, goddamnit!
**LEFT!**

YAY! Time to decorate!

Even though my parents still fought, sometimes even more than usual, Christmas was my favorite time of year. We at least did things together.
Do you remember these ones were mine when I was a kid?
INDY
We felt closer. Like a family.

Hm hm
hm hm
I'LL HAVE A BLUE CHRISTMAS

Where's the checkbook?
Mine's in my purse.
Where's yours?

I must have left it at work.
I have a bill to pay.

Don't forget to write down the amount.

Say, did you pick up those presents I suggested for the kids?
I didn't have time.

Do you think you could—
LISTEN!
I'm **busy** at work! How can you expect me to do the shopping when I'm working my **butt off** all day?!
INDYSOC

THAT'S YOUR JOB!

We need to leave for Dad's work party in thirty minutes.

Let's finish getting ready—hurry up! And don't forget to pick out a toy to keep you busy!

C'mon, hurry up!
The traffic is probably terrible—we'll be late!

Oh—I wrote a couple other checks this week for lunch.
You have to let me know right away when you write a check.
Otherwise I can't keep the account balanced!

That's what I **am** doing **right now!** Okay?!
Why do you have to be like this?

I was just making a point. If it's such a problem, why don't **you** take over managing the finances?!

Managing the house and finances is **your** job! We've been over this a million times!
JERK
SWERVE
SWERVE
SKREETCH
Well, it's hard to do "my job" when I also work and you don't tell me right away when you spend money!

Hi!
Merry Christmas!
Welcome!
So nice to see you!

Oh your place looks lovely!
Welcome, Pages!

Mom! I have to go to the bathroom bad!
Okay—it's just over there.

NNNGH!

OWIE!

MOOOOM

I think your son needs you in the bathroom!

Tyler? Are you okay?
It hurts when I poop. Really bad!

Is it better now?
Yeah, sorry...

You're probably not getting enough fiber.
Or it's a side effect of the Ritalin...

I can't do anything about it now.
Try to drink a lot of water.
Okay.

HA HA HA HA HA HA HA
Why don't we go find the other kids for you to play with.

BUS
OOL BUS

Hey—what's going on with you?

We read a story today about wild rabbits.
And then at recess Casey jumped off the top of the slide.
We thought he was dead but he wasn't.
And then on the way home a girl on the bus was showing off her Walkman!
And it was really cool and I want one. Hers had fuzzy orange head-phones.

You need to settle down. Why don't you have a snack and watch some cartoons.
And she had a Madonna tape but JD said that was lame and everyone started singing Guns 'N Roses.

TRANS-FORMERS MORE THAN MEETS THE EYE
Is Dr. Rogers available?
Yes, I'll wait.

Ah, hello, Doctor...
I'm sorry to bother you but—
Yes, yes that's right.

I spoke with Tyler's group counselor this morning.
He said Tyler seems to be getting a little more out of control again.
WAIT
ROO
Well, it's right after school, so he's not had his 4 pm pill yet.

But even when he does get it on time, after school he's still a little wild. **And** having such a hard time falling asleep.
Mm-hmm.

It's like the Ritalin isn't working all of a sudden.

I think what's happening here is what we call the "rebound effect."

The Ritalin doesn't stay in his system very long.
So at the end of the day his body is "bouncing back" from the medicine and worsening the symptoms.

What can we **do**?
It's been like this for a couple weeks now, and it felt like things had gotten so much better...

Try not to worry. This is totally normal and not unexpected.

I think what we need to do is increase his 4 pm dose to ten milligrams.
That should also help with him falling asleep.

He'll still have some medicine in his system to help him calm down and sleep.
Okay.

I'll start giving him a whole ten milligrams tomorrow and see how it goes.
Give it a week and call me back if things don't improve.

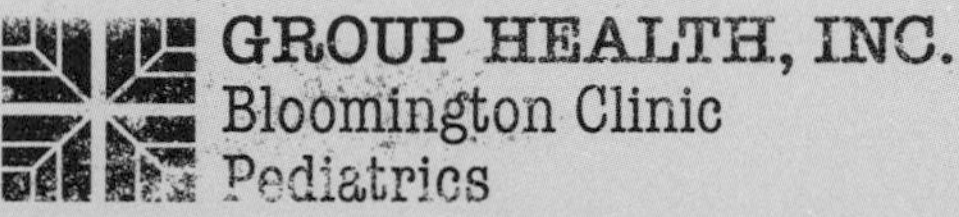

GROUP HEALTH, INC.
Bloomington Clinic
Pediatrics

PATIENT INFO

3434 70 34

PAGE, TYLER M

12 07 76

PATIENT VISIT SUMMARY

Describe according to SOAP
-SUBJECTIVE
-OBJECTIVE
-ASSESSMENT
-PLAN

S: Phone conversation. Tyler's mother called and said he's on Ritalin SR 20mg in the morning and 5mg at about 4pm. His schoolwork is much better and behavior at home is much better except that he seems to be a little bit hyper at home in the afternoon. At bedtime he's having real trouble getting to sleep before 11pm

The counselors at his group said he was hyper in the afternoon. They are seeing him around 4pm at an afterschool group when he hadn't gotten his 4pm medicine.

A: Trouble sleeping, probably because coming off afternoon Ritalin.

P: We're going to increase him to 10mg at 4pm. I think the higher amount will give him a better effect for the evening and he should still have some more in his system when it comes to bedtime and be able to get to sleep.

Problem: TROUBLE SLEEPING. PROBABLY BECAUSE COMING OFF RITALIN.

Signature:

Owen Rogers, M.D./tag

GROUP HEALTH PROGRESS NOTES PLAN, INC.

Later that spring.
And the count on Hrbek is two and one as the pitcher winds up.

What is all this stuff?
Did you take your afternoon medicine?
A line drive!

I did.
I'm doing the taxes.
What's that?

It's money we pay the government so we can have public services like roads, schools, and libraries.

Oh, and this is all the tax stuff?
**GAH!** Don't **touch!** I've got this all organized.

They're receipts and bills and things we paid over the year. I have to go through them all to figure out how much money we owe.
That doesn't seem very fun.

It's not, but it's how we pay for those public services. Plus, you can do things like deductions.
What's a deduction?

It's where you get credit for something—like we get credit for you and your brother, for when we spend money on certain things like the doctor...
Huh, that's—

KRINK

WHEATIES
WHUDD

GODDDAMM SUNNUVVA

#@$!!#@ $#@#!

Why don't you go watch TV in the family room...
SMASH
CRASH

SWEAR YELL CRASH
KICK CRUNCH SMASH

I was scared. I didn't understand why he was like this.
Stop it! You're scaring the children!
#$@!#$@ $@#$

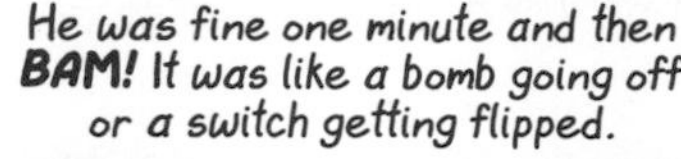
He was fine one minute and then **BAM!** It was like a bomb going off or a switch getting flipped.

EERIE SILENCE
LOOK

SOB

WHEATIES

I'm **so** sorry!
SOB
I didn't mean to get so mad.
I want to make sure you know I love you guys and Mom.
I'm not sure why I get so mad and lose control.
It's like a switch flips in my head.
I'm sorry!
SOB
It's not your fault.
SOB

I just want him to disappear.

The next day.
I just don't know if I can keep doing this.

He's scaring the children. You never know what will set him off. It's like living on a **volcano!**

And it gets **me** so worked up.
I hate it!
**I hate it!**

I know.
I know.
**But...**
I know.
You're right.

But...he's my husband. This is my family.

Oh.

Just getting a snack.
Oh, uh... that's fine.

♫ Hm hm hm ♫
That's...great to hear Jan is doing better.

Mom? I just...

What am I supposed to do?

Back at the doctor.
And he wrote this book report?
Yes!

It's very good for a kid his age. Quite excellent, actually.
I'm not surprised. He **is** very smart.

And from what I gather, his teachers are all happy with his progress as well?
Yes, they seem to be.

And after a few days of the ten milligrams at 4 pm he started getting to sleep much better. I really think it helped.

Good. Given his progress, we might consider giving him a medication break over the summer.
Then again...

He has had problems at home, too, so it might be better if he stays on it.
Yes, I think that would be best.

We also want to watch him for signs of tolerance to the Ritalin. If that happens, we've got some other meds we could look at.
Okay.

Tyler?
How about you? How have you been feeling?
I feel fine.

Well, good, I think we can just see you back here in six months unless something comes up before then.

C'mon, Tyler.
Time to go!

What?
Oh, okay!

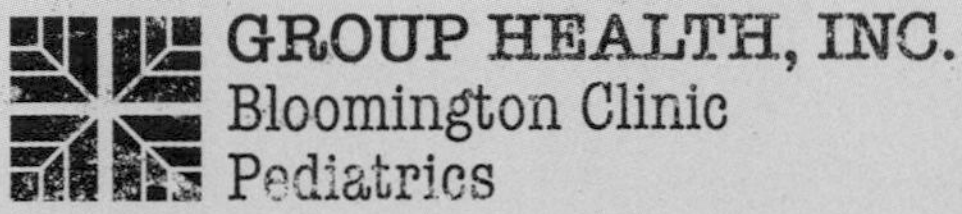

# GROUP HEALTH, INC.
Bloomington Clinic
Pediatrics

PATIENT INFO

3434 70 34

PAGE, TYLER M

12 07 76

PATIENT VISIT SUMMARY

Describe according to SOAP
-SUBJECTIVE
-OBJECTIVE
-ASSESSMENT
-PLAN

S: F/U Ritalin. Tyler's been doing quite well. School progress is excellent. Teachers are very pleased with his performance. He finished his group and the counselors didn't feel he needs more group work. The Ritalin is 20mg in the morning and 10mg at 4pm. After a few days of the 4pm Ritalin 10mg dose he started sleeping better at night.

O: Alert and happy. He showed me a book report that he had just written, which was quite good, actually excellent for his age.

A: Attention deficit, improved on Ritalin.

P: Continue the Ritalin 20mg SR in the morning and 10mg in the afternoon. We'll see him again in about 6 months. He takes it every day including weekends. Might think about stopping over the summer though he's had behavior problems at home as well. If he does develop some tolerance to the Ritalin we might consider switching to imipramine or Cylert.

Problem:

Signature:

Owen Rogers, M.D./tag

GROUP HEALTH PROGRESS NOTES PLAN, INC.

At the start of summer, a new family moved in across the street.
Hi! We're the Ahlbergs.
We just moved here from Sweden.
I'm Kris, and this is Emily and Jon.
Welcome to the neighborhood!
Hi!

It was great having a kid my age right across the street.
We moved here because of my mom's job.
Wow! I can't imagine moving so far away.

We immediately started hanging out almost every day.
Does everyone here have a Nintendo?
My cousin did.
Most people. But I have a SEGA.

How come?
My parents thought it was better.
It's still fun.

*Super Mario* is okay, but I really like building models.
Do you?
Sorta.

My dad gets them for me sometimes. But I'm not very good with the glue.
Heh heh.

And I always ruin the decals.
M

I just started on this kit when we were at my cousin's in Delaware.
It's a P-38 Lightning.
Ooh, just like in 1943!

Huh?
It's a video game. They have one at the arcade.
I'll show you sometime.

Want to work on this with me?
Sure!

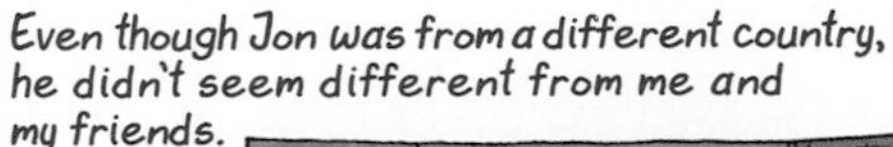
Even though Jon was from a different country, he didn't seem different from me and my friends.

SPLOOOSH

Well, not **that** different.
Does Tyler want to stay for dinner?
We're having pickled herring!
Uh... I think my mom was making something special tonight. Thanks, though!

Eventually Jon was just another friend, finding ways to pass the long, endless days of summer.

Okay—now just move it a little...

**Jon!** It's time to come in!

See you tomorrow!
Oh! We're leaving to go camping in the morning!

We'll be back next week.
Okay, see ya!

Our annual camping trip marked the end of summer, but it was something I looked forward to every year.
Car's packed!
Don't forget the Twizzlers!
WHUD
We'll get up at 5 am so we can get on the road early and be in Duluth for breakfast!

DULUTH
35

Ooh—look at that!
Z
Z

'65 Mustang... That's the kind of car I want someday.
62
I could go racing with the vintage club!

pfft What, when we win the lottery?

Of course, there were still things for my dad to get mad about.
Who ate all the #@!$ Twizzlers?!

SNAP
#$!@
Piece of goddamn #@!$

#$ @!# $!$ $@$ !#@ $!# @

But there's the lake, the rocks, the hiking. The total freedom.

There was something new and interesting to discover or remember **everywhere**.

Like Christmas, this was one of the few times we came together and felt like a family. Close.

The call was coming from **inside the house!**

The new school year brought new challenges like switching classrooms.
BBBRRIIIIIIINGGG

Let's get chapter two done for tomorrow, okay?

Get seated, everyone.
We're going to start reading a book called *Watership Down.*

We'll do some reading in class, but you'll be able to take this home, too.
Um...I forgot—

Yes, Tyler, what is it?
I forgot my math assignment next door.

Ms. Beverly wrote it on the board, and I forgot to copy it down.
You'll need to get that later. We're doing something else now.

Tyler?
Please, take your seat. We need to get going on this.

But I won't know what I'm supposed to do for my homework!

It's fine. You can go look after we're done here, okay?

But I forgot.
Should we make some more Weird Al music videos tonight?
Yeah!

The next day.
Okay—let's get out your chapter two work and look it over.

Oh no!

Yes, Tyler?
Uh...

I forgot to write down the assignment, and then I forgot all about it.

You can turn it in tomorrow if you like.
sigh
**With** the next chapter's work!

Eventually I learned to write down my assignments as soon as they were written on the board.
Chapter 5
15-21
35-47
scribble
scribble

And I got the hang of the "room switching" routine.

Things were going pretty well.
For my *Watership Down* bio, I picked Blackberry because I am clever and good at figuring out how things work.
Watership
Down
Present

Until one day...
Hurry up! You're going to miss the bus!

I'm coming!

Tyler, sit down!

HA HA HA HA
HA HA HA

I already told you to **sit down.**

Tyler, do you know the answer?
What? Huh?

DUUUUUUUH
HA HA
HA
HA
HA HA HA
HA HA
HA
MILK

CACKLE CACKLE
That's ***it!*** Out in the hall ***now!***

Yes, this is Mrs. Page...

What **the heck** is wrong with Tyler today?!

He... He must have forgotten to take his medicine this morning.

I am **so** sorry!

I'm just shocked at how different he's been today.
He's like a totally different person!
Well, the medicine he's on helps him control his impulsive behavior.

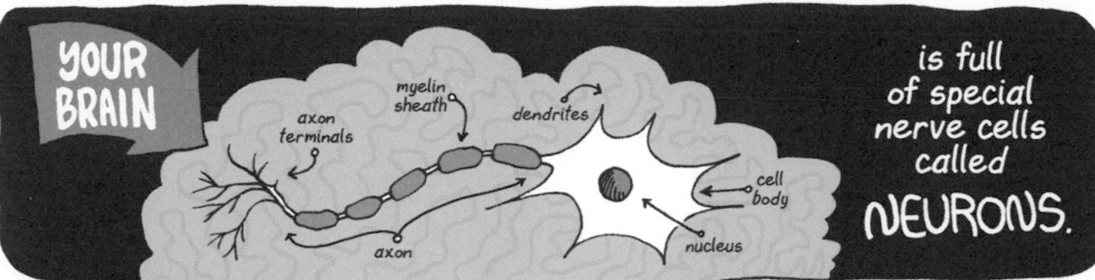

YOUR BRAIN
axon terminals
myelin sheath
dendrites
cell body
axon
nucleus
is full of special nerve cells called NEURONS.

They pass along weak electro-chemical signals that generate our thoughts, memories, feelings, and actions.
Mmm—I want a sandwich.

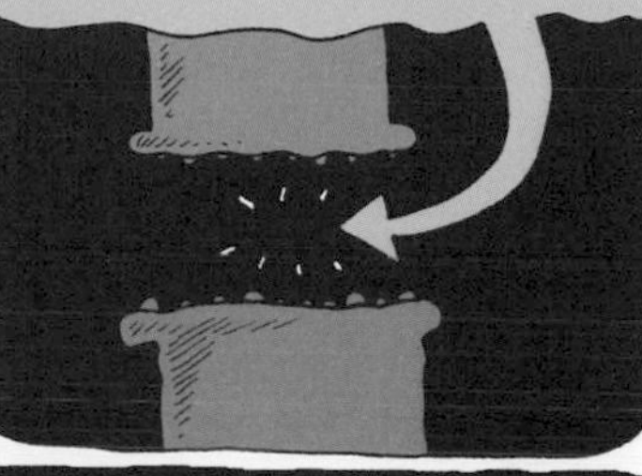

But the neurons don't touch each other. They're separated by a small space called a synapse or snyaptic gap.

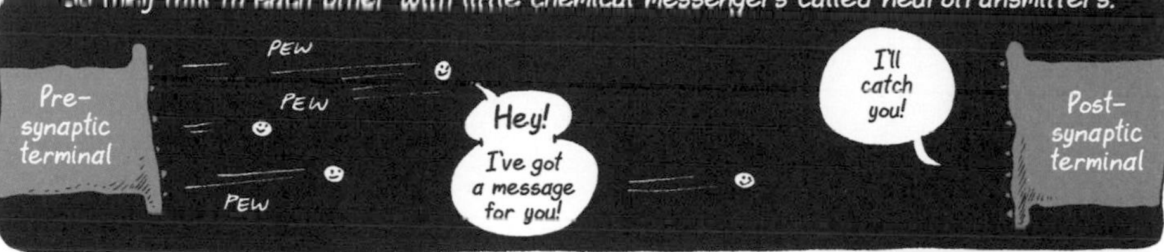

So they talk to each other with little chemical messengers called neurotransmitters.
PEW
PEW
PEW
Pre-synaptic terminal
Hey! I've got a message for you!
I'll catch you!
Post-synaptic terminal

In the most simplistic sense, Ritalin and other ADHD meds act on the dopamine, norepinephrine, and serotonin neurotransmitter pathways in the brain.

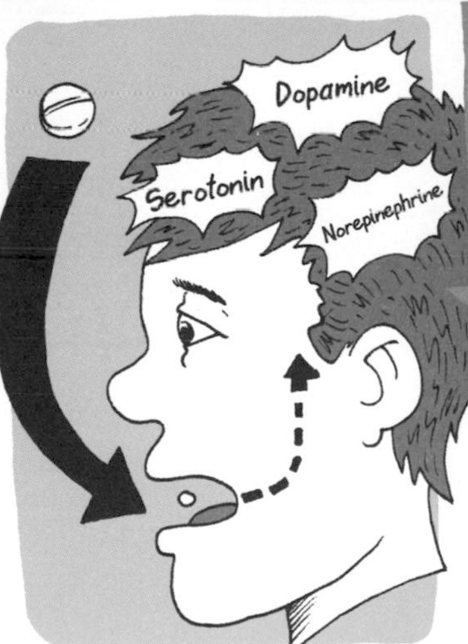


And these pathways control the very brain areas responsible for the functions ADHDers are deficient in.

- attention
- planning
- focus
- short-term memory
- task management
- cross-temporal association

-SO-
my brain doesn't have enough dopamine or serotonin or whatever?
It's not that SIMPLE.
Your brain is **very** complex.
I'm sorry I'm so complicated...
100 billion neurons!
You can't just take dopamine or serotonin pills.
Not a thing
DOPEX
DOPAMINE TABLETS
25mg

If it were that easy, ADHD meds would completely cure symptoms when taken, but they don't.
He still has trouble controlling his impulses.
I see.
ADHD meds are **NOT** neurotransmitters. They are **INTERMEDIARY AGENTS** that cause a change in neurotransmitter function and behavior.
OOH!
That Ritalin makes me want to leave dopamine in my synapses longer!

ADHD meds are kind of like glasses for your brain.
Better!

They help you better control your actions and behaviors while you grow and mature, and learn to master your own body.
I think I'm getting the hang of this!

The next day.
I found this old Tylenol tin and put a few of your pills in it.
You can keep it in your backpack in case you forget your medicine again.
Okay.
BALL STATE

But remember—you **only** take it once in the morning. It's **not** candy.
I know, Mom.

And you already took it this morning?
I did.

Missing that pill yesterday showed me something.

For the first time since I'd started taking the Ritalin, I saw how it helped me.

I knew that I had felt different yesterday. I felt out of control.

It was like everything was happening to another person, and I was just watching.

And I didn't understand why that other version of me was doing those things.

That would be one of only a few times I would forget to take my Ritalin.
375
x 482
40

Tyler, I'm giving you a gold star for being so well-behaved today!
12

But while my medicine was definitely helping, and things were pretty good for me, my parents continued to have their problems.

All you do is lay on the couch and read the paper!

What happened to finishing the boys' rooms?
I'm tired, **okay?**

I thought... I thought this new medication was helping you?!

TRIBUNE

It was, but...
then it wasn't.

SNAP
STAR TRI
OKAY?!

I stopped taking it a few weeks ago. It was making me tired all the time!
CRUNCH

GET OFF MY **BACK!**

I can't keep doing this! I thought you were getting better!

You're **supposed** to be helping me with the Christmas budget!

I just told you we can't spend as much this year!
CRUMPLE
But what does that **mean?!**

YELL

YELL

NOD
NOD

YELL
SCREAM
SHOUT
SWEAR

Hey, heh heh, look—
Cheers is on!
CLICK
YELL
YELL
YELL

Hey,
Cliffy!
YELL
SCREAM
SWEAR

YELL
PUNCH
PUNCH
PUNCH

Was that...?
No, it couldn't
be...

EERIE
SILENCE

SNEAK
SNEAK
SNEAK

SOB

SOB
SOB

SLAM

The next day.
TETTEGOUCHE
STATE PARK

What happened to the wall?
...
...Your father...

Hmmm...
TETTEGOUCHE
STATE PARK

C'mere, sweetie...

What do you think about spending Christmas at the farm in Indiana this year?
TETTEGOUCHE

Just you, me, and your brother...

Yes.

Okay.
Why don't you go get a snack and play.
PAT PAT
TETTEGOUCHE

She didn't tell me not to tell my dad. But I knew this was a chance to get away from... whatever was happening here.

A few days later.
Now we're not going to be able to take **all** the presents with us.
Do we **have** to go?

Santa will still come to the farm, though. Don't worry!
Yay!

Honey, I know this is confusing. I'm sorry, but...

I need to be away from your dad for a little while. I think you do, too.

It's okay. I know.
Dad **is** such a meanie!

Your uncle Randy will be here soon to get us.
Uncle Randy!
Yay!

Why don't you both go make some drawings for Dad.
So he has... something.

He's going to be furious when we're not here...

Can I really do this?

Soon.
Hey, y'all!
MOTO

UNCLE RANDY!

Sounds like you kids are gonna spend Christmas at the farm with Grandma an' me an' your aunt!
We can't wait.
Yay!
MOTO

What ya kids got here?
Making some drawings?
MOTO

Mom said we should leave something for Dad.

You're MEAN

we're leaving!

Merry Christmas -tyler

Sis—I can't tell you how happy I am you called.
MOTO

We **all** are. Everyone at home is just waiting with open arms!
MOTO

HUG

MOTO

I...

MOTO
I... I can't do this, Randy. I'm sorry.

WHUT?

I'm sorry!
SOB SOB SOB

I'm sorry I made you drive all this way. I just...
MOTO

When it comes down to it, I can't go. This is my family.
My home.
My husband.

But, sis, you're miserable! You told Mom yourself!

You called me in tears the other day screaming, saying you had to get out of here.

I just drove **fourteen hours** to get here!
I know, I know, I'm sorry!

I can pay for a hotel...

No.
I'm not staying.

This is your last chance.
PLEASE?
For the kids?

I can't.
I'm sorry.

SLAM

Boys... we...
I changed my mind.

WHAT?!

I just... It didn't feel right not to have Christmas here.

Maybe next year?

...
...Can I put the presents back?

I didn't understand. We were going to get away.

It was going to be different...better.

Who wants egg nog?!

Maybe it would have been weird to leave...

Christmas and New Year's came and went.
TMNT

It was like the possibility of going to Indiana never happened.
RUDE
HAPPY
NEW YEAR

We played with our new toys, had snowball fights, went sledding and ice skating.

Everything was like it was, like we all had amnesia.
STARTIM

I was even back at the doctor.
More trouble sleeping, huh?
And he's having trouble winding down again.

We have some options. This is a frequent enough problem we can consider another medication, as I've mentioned before.

The medication your husband is currently on, imipramine, might help.
I thought that was an anti-depressant?

It is. But at very low doses it can cause drowsiness.

So it is often used as a sleep aid in cases like this.

By the way—how are things at home, with Tyler's father?

Better I guess?
Okay at least.

He finally went back to the doctor, got on the imipramine like you said...

It's been a couple months now. He seems a lot better. He even said so himself.

Well, that's good. I'm glad to hear that. I know it's a struggle.
SIGH

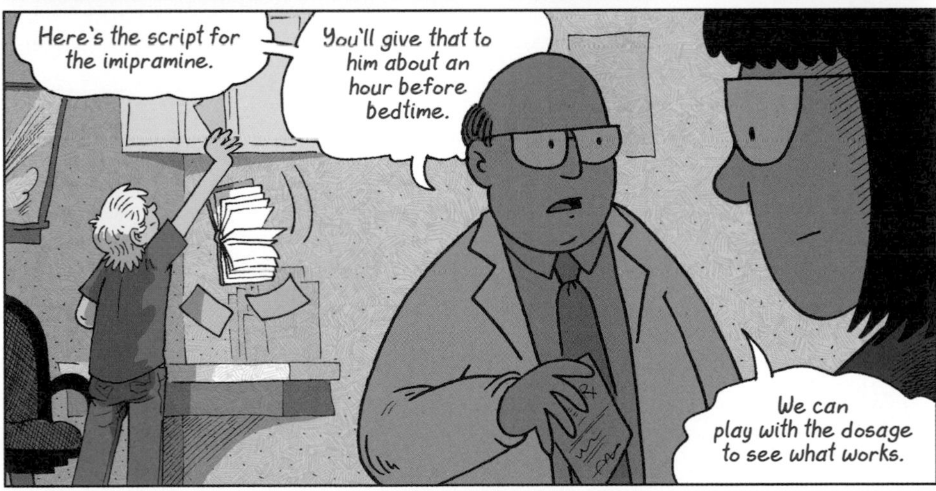
Here's the script for the imipramine.
You'll give that to him about an hour before bedtime.
We can play with the dosage to see what works.

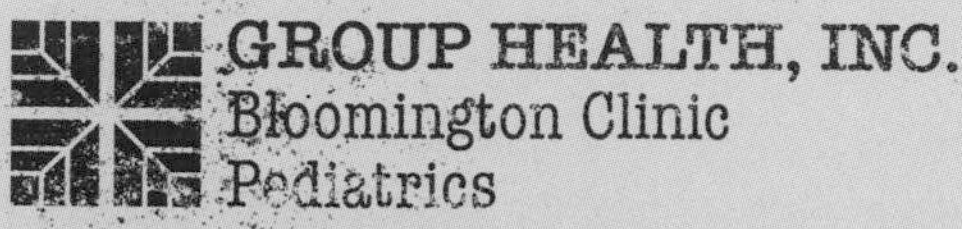

GROUP HEALTH, INC.
Bloomington Clinic
Pediatrics

PATIENT INFO

3434 70 34

PAGE, TYLER M

12 07 76

PATIENT VISIT SUMMARY

Describe according to SOAP
-SUBJECTIVE
-OBJECTIVE
-ASSESSMENT
-PLAN

S: Ritalin check. Tyler has different teachers now for math and English. He says that going from room to room makes it a little harder for him. Sometimes an assignment is written on the board in the other room and if he's not gotten it done he can't use extra time in the other room to do it. He likes reading best. It is hard to concentrate in the classroom. When he takes work home he is able to get it done quickly.

When he missed his Ritalin one day the teacher noticed immediately that he had real trouble settling down. He tends to be very disorganized, too, forgetting what he has to do.

Taking 20mg SR Ritalin in the morning, 10mg in the afternoon. Still trouble getting to sleep.

O: Tyler was in almost constant motion during the exam. Okay physically otherwise.

A: Attention deficit disorder. Some tolerance to Ritalin?

P: We talked about the various options—increasing Ritalin, switching to Cylert or possibly adding imipramine. We decided to add imipramine, starting w/ dose of 10mg about an hour before bed. Can go up to 20mg or 30mg after a few days if he's still not getting to sleep faster. We'll see him back here in 2 weeks for a check.

Problem: ATTENTION DEFICIT DISORDER. STOMACHACHES AND CONSTIPATION, TROUBLE SLEEPING. SOME TOLERANCE TO RITALIN.

Signature:

Owen Rogers, M.D./tag

GROUP HEALTH PROGRESS NOTES PLAN, INC.

The next day.
Dr. Rogers wants you to take this other pill before bedtime.
He thinks it will help you sleep.
BRUSH BRUSH
Okay.


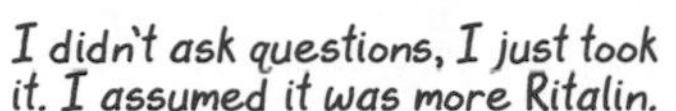

I didn't ask questions, I just took it. I assumed it was more Ritalin.

After a few days, it seemed to be helping.
Z

But I woke up feeling groggy...
Huh?

...so I didn't take it for very long.
I said—don't forget to take your medicine.
Oh right.

And while I was doing well in school...
Here are your report cards.

Very good, Tyler.
NAME Tyler Page
MINNEAPOLIS PUBLIC SCHOOLS
MINNEAPOLIS
MINNESOTA
HABITS AND ATTITUDES
Period 1 2 3
Participates only when encouraged
Participates with confidence
Needs to develop self-control
Often withdraws from the group
Shows qualities of leadership
Accepts helpful criticism
Improving
Better
GROWTH IN INDEPENDENCE
Makes good use of time
Accepts and completes responsibilities
Needs help/encouragement to complete tasks
Is able to work independently
Meets new situations well
Better
WORK HABITS
Is reasonably accurate in following directions
Needs help in following directions
Is easily distracted
Works consistently and carefully
Improving
SAFETY PRACTICES
Accepts and usually follows safety rules
Shows little regard for personal safety

...I still managed to do my fair share of dumb things.
I think that old train set is down here somewhere...

Maybe it's up—

Ooh!
PHOTO ELECTRIC FOOTBALL
What is it?

A dart!

ZIIIIIP

THUNK

Isn't this cool?
Let's go throw it at stuff outside!

YAH!
THUNK

I could be like a dart ninja or something!
I thought we were looking for your dad's old train set?

As was often the case, I found something new and became obsessed with it.

ZIIIP
CRACK
CRAAAAAAAAAAACKLE

OH MY GOD OH MY GOD OH MY GOD OH MY GOD OH MY GOD OH MY GOD

GLANCE

What do I do?!
How do I—
PANT PANT PANT

I walked in circles in a neighbor's yard for almost an hour.
What am I going to do?
They know I've been playing with the dart.
What else would have done it? A rock? A bird?
What else could I tell them?

I guess I have to go face them.
I can't blame something else. What's going to happen?

...I suppose you saw what I did...?
Lucky for you it's safety glass, so it didn't fall out.

You're going to help fix it and pay for the cost.
What about the dart?
Can I have it back?

Go to your room before your father gets home!
SLAM
I wish I could have my dart back...

And where the **hell** have you been?!

NO
Don't—it was an accident!

SCREEEEEE
EE
EAM

SLAM
SCREAM

You're only making it worse!
SCREAM

WAKWAKWAKWAKWAK
SCREAM!

SOB
SOB SOB
SOB

WAAAHUHUUUWAAAAAWAH

I wasn't crying because it hurt but because I was terrified.

It was always like that.

The thing was, no matter how many times I was grounded or spanked or punished? It never mattered.
SNIFF
SNIFF

I still did exactly whatever I wanted or whatever dumb thing popped into my head.

It was like I forgot about all the times before.
SNAP

GO TO YOUR ROOM!

YOU'RE GROUNDED FOR A WEEK!

WHEATIES

SPANK
SPANK
SPANK

It was almost like I couldn't make the connection between my bad behavior and the consequences of punishment.

ADHD IS OFTEN DESCRIBED AS

# TIME BLINDNESS

I can't see!

THE IMPULSIVE AND RANDOM BEHAVIOR **AND** INABILITY TO LEARN FROM MISTAKES

IS OFTEN SAID TO BE DUE TO:

AN INABILITY TO KNIT TOGETHER EXPERIENCES AND BEHAVIORS ACROSS TIME

(AMONG OTHER THINGS).

This is called "cross-temporal association" and is a key function of the prefrontal cortex.

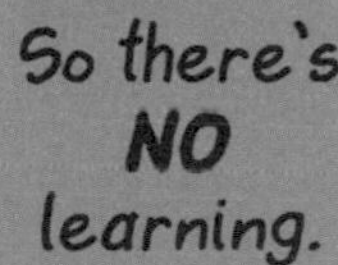

We don't stop and think before we do things.

And once we've done something, there's no bridge between the initiation of the behavior and of the outcomes.

So there's **NO** learning.

Hi!
INITIATION POINT

**NO CONNECTION**

Who are you?
OUTCOME OVERLOOK

After some trial and error, I got dialed in on a Ritalin routine that seemed to work pretty well for me.
20mg SR* at 8 am
10mg at 4 pm
5mg at 6 pm
*Sustained Release

And school was going great.
Tyler is testing well into the high school level in his reading and writing.
I **knew** he was smart!
That's great!

But I was still doing my fair share of impulsive things at home.

You stole the brakes off my bike!
**What?!** You never even ride your bike!

You ate all my candy!
'o I 'idn't!

Who ate all the Oreos? We just got these!

But nothing really "harmful."
Ow—he hit me!
Stop it!
What is **wrong** with you two?!
He hit **me!**

My sense of self-awareness was growing, too. I found myself thinking more about my family, and the doctor visits, and the pills I took. What ***was*** going on with me?

Then one evening I heard something that started to make sense of it all.

It's not known exactly what causes this syndrome. Some say it's due to mothers smoking during pregnancy. Others say it's genetic.

Whatever causes it, doctors are treating it with a drug called Ritalin.
It's really amazing how well Ritalin treats this problem.

I've had two of these kids in my class recently.
They were sweet boys but would just fidget and run around all day.
SCHOOL
Once they started treatment, they became model students.

They're talking about me! Is that what I have? "Attention Deficit Disorder"?
I guess that's what I'm taking the Ritalin for.

But...does that mean there's something wrong with me?
I don't feel **sick.**
What does it mean?

LABELS
CAN BE A GOOD THING OR A BAD THING.
You have ADHD?!
No way!
Yeah!

We have a history of applying labels to things in order to better understand them by categorizing, comparing, and describing.

Periodic Table of Elements

A diagnostic label like ADHD can be helpful because it recognizes your symptoms and/or suffering.

The label confers legitimacy.

See?! ADHD is **not** fake!
DSM

The *diagnosis* says:

Yes—this is real!

Thus labeled, you can set forth on a path of understanding and treatment.

Wow—this sounds exactly like me!
DSM

The label has allowed us to document, describe, and refine our understanding of ADHD, including research.

What about the prepotent response?
Ah yes!

## BUT: LABELS CAN ALSO BE HARMFUL FOR TWO MAIN REASONS:

**1** **A LABEL IS A CATCHALL AND IS TOO-EASILY APPLIED TO ANYONE APPEARING TO HAVE THE BASIC SYMPTOMS OF A DISORDER OR DISEASE (WHICH MOST PEOPLE HAVE FROM TIME TO TIME).**

Anyone feeling scatterbrained is "**ADHD.**"

Anyone feeling sad is "**DEPRESSED.**"

**THESE LABELS CAN BE USED TOO EASILY.**

Some experts believe we overdiagnose ADHD by 20–30% because it's too easy—and clinicians are lazy, not well trained, etc.

Conversely, many who would benefit from a diagnosis never get it—underdiagnosis.

**2** **LABELS CAN CARRY A STIGMA.**

It is easy for a person to self-identify with a label, especially the negative aspects, which can affect their self-esteem and self-image.

I can't do this because of my ADHD!

The label didn't mean much to me because my parents and doctor didn't use it. Though once I heard the term, I began noticing it used more at school and in the media.

Whether or not I use the label, the ADHD is there no matter what.

The application of any label, particularly a medical diagnosis, should be done with the most careful consideration. (Especially in children!)

It had been a year since Jon moved into the neighborhood, so he was no longer the "new kid."

But as he got comfortable with his new life, he became disruptive to mine.

TAG! You're it!
WHAT?!

RUN RUN RUN

Missed!
HA HA HA
SWIPE

TAG!

He'll never catch us!

He's too fat!

GRRRRRRR

GAH!
HA!
SWIPE

Arrgh!
WHIFF

TOO SLOW!
WHIFF

GET BACK HERE!
SWIPE

HA HA
You're too slow and fat to catch us!
Am not!

SHUT UP!

ALMOST!

SWIPE
SLORP
Missed again!

SWIPE
GRAH!

BUUUUUSS!
BUS

HUFF
HUFF
Told you you're too slow!

Oh no!
I must have stepped on my juice box!
SQUISH

I'm **so** mad at Jon!
HUFF
HUFF

I feel like I'm going to **explode!**

FUME FUME

POOF
LYNDALE
MIDDLE
SCHOOL

It was almost like I had emotional amnesia.
Did you see Ninja Turtles yesterday?
Ha ha!
Yeah—wasn't Shredder hilarious?!

I was so mad at him and click like a switch it was gone...

Kind of like how I am with my brother sometimes. We could be messing around...

And he'll hit me accidentally and click I'm like the Hulk.
existentia

It was like a switch I didn't have the control for.
Just like...Dad.

# EMOTIONAL REGULATION IS

something else ADHDers can struggle with

our ability to regulate or "downshift" our emotions and emotional responses.

This is a crucial part of social behavior!

It develops as we age, residing in our frontal lobes, which aren't fully mature until our mid to late 20s (and later in ADHDers).

As babies we express all emotions openly. But as we grow older, emotional regulation helps us process our feelings internally.

This skill develops along with our **VERBAL** and **NONVERBAL WORKING MEMORY** executive functions as we learn to "talk" to ourselves.

I'm really hungry.

WOW — that lady is really ugly!

I have to pee!

It's a good thing I don't say this stuff out loud!

Emotional Regulation is like our internal "traffic cop" who helps modulate our behaviors. It is one of the **EXECUTIVE FUNCTIONS** ADHDers are deficient in.

Just a minute....

Where are you going?

INSULTING COMMENT

This is an aspect of ADHD that hasn't been included in the official diagnostic criteria, but is now understood by most clinicians as another cornerstone of ADHD.

And as much as I disliked when I felt or behaved impulsively, it was something I would still struggle with occasionally even on medication.

It also reminded me of when my parents fought...

It's crazy and scary...
DAVANNIS

...and when it's over, it was like it never happened.

What's wrong with Mom and Dad?
I think they were fighting last night.

How was I expected to work on my self-control when Dad was always modeling the opposite behavior, often in very frightening ways?

Our house was littered with the reminders of their fights and Dad's tantrums.

STOP IT

SMASH

STOP IT

STOP IT

SOB SOB SOB

...

SLAM
FVOP
uhuuuhuuh huh huuuuh

I love my parents.
They are my parents after all.
They take care of me.
And they've tried to make a nice home for us.
But I wish they'd just get divorced!

I hate it. I hate it. I hate it.
They both yell and scream, but it almost always starts with Dad.
He's like a big baby.
And I'm sick of it.
Sick of what it does to Mom—mentally and physically...
But most of all, I'm sick of seeing it in me.

LYNDALE MIDDLE SCHOOL
All right, everyone, listen up!

We've been talking about alliteration all morning.
So I want you to partner up...
Alliteration

And write a short poem using as much alliteration as possible.
Then we'll read them!

Hey—wanna work together?
Sure!

What should we do?
Hmm
How about...uh... "Pete's pig" something?

whisper whisper
whisper

HA HA HA HA HA HA

giggle
giggle
giggle

HA HA HA HA HA HA HA HA

Okay, let's wrap it up. One more minute!
HA HA HA

Who wants to go first?
This is the funniest thing ever!

This better be good.
Ahem.
giggle giggle

Pete punched Paul—
BWAH-HAHA
HA HA HA HA

—in his precious penis prior to Paul puking on Pete's prize-winning pig.
AHAHAHA SQUEEEEEL HAHAHA

HA HA HA HA HAHAHA

Can't... stop...
Oh this hurts!
Oh God, I can't control it!

Is he okay?
HA HA HA HA HA HA

Oh my God—they're all looking at me. They think I'm hilarious!

HA HA HA HA
Okay, Tyler, yes, it's very funny, but that's enough.
This is great!

HA HA HA HA
OOF
Heh heh.

Ahahaha
SIGH
Oh man...
What a weirdo!

All right, do I dare ask who's next?
It wasn't even that funny.
What's wrong with him?

Later.
US CO.

You wanna do something?

Nah...
I've uh... got a lot of homework.

Okay.
See ya!

I'll have to remember that poem!

Ooh—a letter from Grandma!

Hey, Mom—you got a letter from Grandma!

Thanks, honey. How was school?

Pretty good.
We wrote a funny poem this morning.

"This can't go on..."

"It's okay to give up on your marriage. Come home to us. We won't judge you."

DuckTales
Woo-ooh!
Race cars, lasers,
Air -O- planes

"You have to think of the children. We're tired of hearing about the fights and the way he treats you and the kids. It's not right."

"Turning away your brother when he came to help was the last straw. Come home, please."

What do we do now, Unca' Scrooge?
SOB

SLAM
I'm home! What's for dinner?

TUCK TUCK

WIPE
WIPE

SMOOOTH

I'll be down in a minute!

NOM NOM NOM

What are you in such a hurry for?
I wanna finish building a table in my treehouse.

Oh? Do you want some help?
Naw, that's okay.

I can find some good nails for you.
I got some.

Found a nice piece of wood in the scrap bin, too!
I can help you measure...

That's okay. I've got it!

Hm hm hm
TAP
TAP
TAP
Stupid nail!
Try a new one...
DANG IT!
SMASH
Steady...
SMASH

ROOAAAR

ARG
WHACK
WHACK
SLAM
SLAM
SLAM
POUND
POUND

GRRRRR

It's stuck!

What am I doing?!
This is just how Dad acts.
I hate when he acts like that.
I don't want to be like that!
It's childish. Like a baby having a tantrum...

I'm not going to be like that ever again.

The next day.

...

Uh... Did you see Simpsons last night?

HA HA—yeah!

I loved when Homer said, "I think he's talking to you!"
Heh heh!

What about Sideshow Bob stepping on all those rakes?!
HA HA yeah!

My vow to control my anger was made easier by the fact I was getting older and more mature, more self-aware.
SUSAN B. ANTHONY SCHOOL

Though I still found ways to get in trouble...
We caught your son writing lewd remarks on our sidewalk with chalk!
I'm so sorry...
SOB

...or get caught up in a moment...
Okay—he's all tied up.
Let's push him down the hill! Heh heh!
HA HA yeah!
That will be hilarious!

...or get carried away with wacky behavior...
Stop it, Tyler! We're trying to play Super Mario!
AUGH—look out! I'm **SO** crazy!
What a **weirdo!**

...or just be dumb.
Hey—
—learning to use a band saw today.
Let me draw something on your face!

No way!
What are you going to do?
REEBOK

Nothing. I promise!
Just hold still.

There!

I have a mustache now, don't I?
HA HA HA

You **butthead!** Now I get to draw on you!
No way!

It's only fair.
I promise it will be small!

I didn't know when to stop.

DRAW DRAW DRAW
DRAW

DRAW DRAW
DRAW DRAW

DRAW
POOP
BUTTS

NATE!
TYLER!
BUTTS
POOP
POOP

What the **heck** are you two doing?!

I'm **trying** to talk to the class here.

Uh... Well...umm... **He** started it!

You **both** get **detention!**

POOP
BEEBOK

GROUP HEALTH
BLOOMINGTON
CLINIC
I think he must have forgotten his medicine that day.

Tyler, what do you think about this detention?
I dunno...

We were just messing around, being silly, not listening, I guess?
Do you think maybe you forgot your medicine that day?

I don't know.
I'm usually really good about remembering.
But... maybe?
Hmm.

And you've **never** had detention before?
No.

It does seem like you really do still need the Ritalin.

I know it might seem at times like you don't want to because you think "taking drugs" is a bad thing, but this isn't like that.
I know.

This is a medicine to help you. Like if your mom gives you Tylenol for a headache or puts disinfectant on a wound.

It's like...you have a **race car brain**. Doesn't it sometimes feel like that?
Yeah.

But your race car brain has regular brakes and steering.

So you have a hard time controlling yourself.
NOD
NOD

I'll be in the middle of doing something before I have time to think about it.

The other day at school was like that.

It's like my brain doesn't have an "on deck" circle. It's just **batter up!**

Honey, you really are doing so well!
Your mother's right.
It's natural to have a little slipup now and then.

I'm just always checking to see if the medication is really still helping you, and I think it's safe to say it is, hm?
Yeah.

Okay. I want to have a word with your mother.
Why don't you wait here.

Let's just step out here...

How have things been at home? With Tyler's father?

SIGH
They're...okay, I guess.

My mother really wants me to leave, take the kids back to Indiana.
I almost did.

But I **couldn't**.
I told her **this** was my home.
sniff

She seems to be supportive of us working on things.
And Tyler's father?

I didn't...
I don't think he knows how close I came to leaving.
He's been on imipramine himself, and it seems to be helping.
He seems less depressed. Less impulsive.
Well, that's good.
Let me know if anything changes.

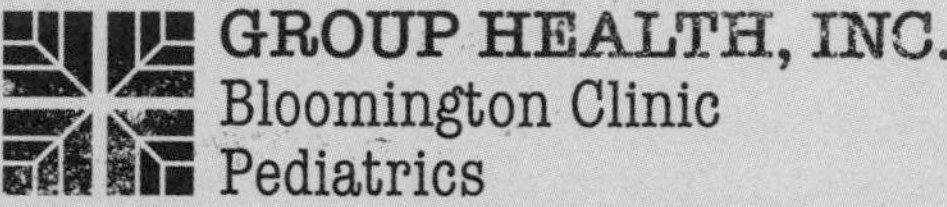

GROUP HEALTH, INC.
Bloomington Clinic
Pediatrics

PATIENT INFO
3434 70 34
PAGE, TYLER M
12 07 76

PATIENT VISIT SUMMARY

Describe according to SOAP
-SUBJECTIVE
-OBJECTIVE
-ASSESSMENT
-PLAN

S: Ritalin check. Tyler's been doing well, though some impulsive behavior. The 6pm dose of 5mg Ritalin is helping with bedtime and sleep though Tyler says his mind races a lot, but it's getting better.

A: ADD, well maintained.

P: Talked again about what the medicine does and how it helps him control himself and he seemed to see that. He's missed it a few times and can see in retrospect how he is different.

Talked about managing his behavior. Mom and Dad will try and sit down w/ him after events to try to talk about how he could have done things differently, recognizing the problem, and thinking of alternative actions.

Tyler does do some foot tapping, which will go on until he's told to stop, self-stimulation.

Things have been better at home. Father seems less depressed and is back on imipramine, which seems to be helping both the depression and impulsivity. I suspect that he does have adult residual ADD.

Mom has written to her own mother stating "this is my home" in response to her mother's letter that she should leave Dad. Mom is hoping her mother will be supportive of her decision.

Problem: ADD ON TREATMENT. .DOING WELL IN SCHOOL.

Signature:
Owen Rogers, M.D./tag

GROUP HEALTH PROGRESS NOTES PLAN, INC.

I clearly still needed the Ritalin.

But I was getting bigger and the same dose wasn't having the effect it used to.

Subconsciously, I was constantly craving stimulation everywhere.
TAP
TAP
TAP
TAP
TAP
TAP
TAP
TAP
TAP
TYLER!
Stop tapping your foot!

TAP
TAP
TAP
TAP
TAP
TAP
TAP
TAP
TAP
TYLER!

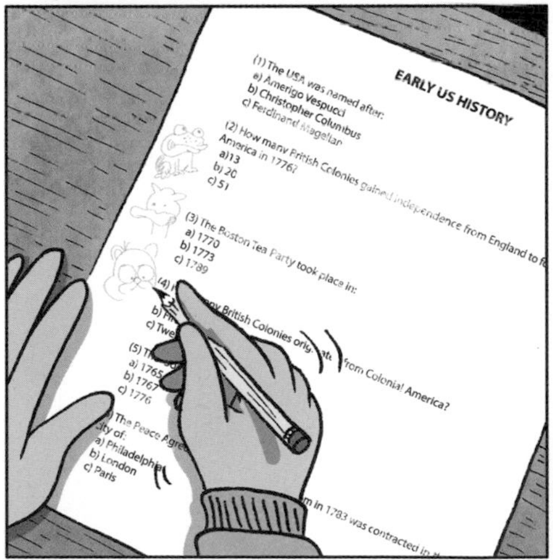
EARLY US HISTORY
(1) The USA was named after:
a) Amerigo Vespucci
b) Christopher Columbus
c) Ferdinand Magellan
a) 13
b) 20
c) 51
(3) The Boston Tea Party took place in:
a) 1770
b) 1773
c) 1789
c) 1776
a) Philadelphia
b) London
c) Paris

I realized drawing while my teachers talked actually helped me pay better attention.

Though of course, some of them didn't understand.

I came up with a lot of good ideas during class.

And started spending more and more of my free time drawing.

Yeah, I did.
Wanna see?
Sure! I want to
know what happens!

Ahahaha,
this is
awesome!

Is that a comic?
Did **you** draw it?
Yeah!

It's this character I came up
with called Steroid Man.
OOH!
Here.

This guy took so many steroids his muscles
won't stop growing. He has to live in a
metal suit or he'll explode.
Sweet!

This is
cool!
Thanks!

Where are you going?
I've got all the tids 'n' bits ready!
The Christmas party at Nate's house.

Oh, I forgot about that.

Be home by nine!

But the easiest place to find stimulation was from food, and at the holidays it was everywhere.
Hey!
I brought cookies!
The hot cider and hot chocolate are ready!
EGG NOG

I didn't conciously think about it...
SCARF
SCARF
SCARF
SCARF

...but I craved "fuel" nonstop.
GLUG GLUG GLUG GLUG GLUG

I know I shouldn't eat more than one but...
Mmm, **so** good!
NOMPF
NOMPF
NOMPF
I can't...stop...

Nobody will notice if I hide the wrappers at the bottom of the garbage.
Hey, c'mon!
SMASH
We're gonna play Pictionary!

And then to make it even worse...
DING DONG
SWELL FOODS

Hi, I'm from Swell Foods. We're a new frozen food delivery service!
Hi!
SWELL CREAM

Would you be interested in trying some of our products?
Oh my...
Look at all this stuff!

Suddenly our freezer was always full of frozen treats and snacks.
ICE CREAM
CONES

I found them irresistible.
ICE CREAM
SUNDAE CONES
DROOL

I'll just have one.

One more is okay...

Just one more...

Once "fueled," I'd shut myself away from the nonsense of my family.
DEW
Maybe I'll call this character Alloy instead of Steroid Man...

Of course, all of this "fueling" and lack of activity began to take its toll on me.

Thankfully the geeks, nerds, and weirdos I was starting to make friends with didn't seem to care much about appearances.

We are the knights who say "Ni!"

HEH HEH Ni!

Ni!

Ni!

All right, you jokers, settle down and get your work done!

In fact, I fit right in.
Muh-muh my BAH-LONA!
You like Weird Al, too?!
Did you know each of the space shuttle main engines produce 350,000 pounds of thrust?!
I think Gandalf—
ATARI

We mostly cared about making one another laugh and having fun.
The answer is always "forty-two"!
HA HA HA
Forty-two!
Picard is way better than Kirk!
Heh heh heh
Do you want to come over this weekend and join our D&D campaign?

Though I began to absorb some of their more mature behaviors by example.
Okay.
Let's get a head start on this research project.
I'll start looking up re-sources.
Uh...I'll... uh...
...start looking at what pictures we could use.

But they also encouraged my immature side too sometimes.
Hey—look! Tyler can draw the Simpsons!
GIJOE

Oh cool! Draw Bart!
Dude—draw Bart pooping on Mr. Burns!
GIJOE
Gross! Okay!

Ew!
Wow—that's **so** good!

HA HA HA HA HA HA HA HA HA HA
GIJOE
Give it more stink lines!

It's a masterpiece!
Okay—draw Marge barfing on Lisa!
GIJOE
You guys are **so** gross!

It felt like I was building my own family, a family of friends, of people I ***wanted*** to be around.

I got this new *Monty Python* tape we should watch!
Ooh— sure!

What are you boys up to?
CHEEZ IT
Stuff.

Well, your dad will be home late. Find something in the fridge to feed yourselves!
Okay, Mom!

...Do your parents ever fight?

Are you kidding?! Yeah!
TRIZKIT
YAYI

I mean, not that often but yeah, they've had some pretty intense shouting matches.
Do you ever worry that...like, they'll get divorced?
CREMO

I dunno. But y'know my mom was married before.
What? Really?

Yeah. Amy's my half sister, from my mom's first marriage.
Gosh, I didn't know that!

C'mon—I wanna see if you can **really** beat Sonic 2 before we watch Monthy Python!
I told you I did!
I almost did it again yesterday.
SEGA
I guess there are things you don't know about most families...

A few days later.
AUGH!
He got me!
KPEW
So close!

But even my friends let me down sometimes, too.
Hey, Tyler—it's your turn!
'Kay!
CHEW

C'mon, **fattie!**

Heheheheheh! Yeah, hurry up, **fattie!**
HA

HA HA HA HA! FATTIE!

Don't call me that, **butthead!**

Oh no—did we hurt your widdle feelings?

HA HA HA HA

You guys are **jerks!**
HA HA
HA HA
HA

Why would they do that?!

Nate's never acted like that before. Len's a bad influence...

It's okay.
I don't need them anyway.

Art is never mean to me.
It never yells or throws things.
Or calls me fat.
DEW

While my parents had their own problems, they did try and encourage my and my brother's interests.
Cool! A new dinosaur model!
Oh wow—an art supply bin!

I became more curious about the process of different kinds of art making.

An airbrush!

And inking nibs!

I began spending as much time learning about art as I was making it.
HOW TO MAKE COMICS
HISTORY OF DC COMICS

I spent more and more time at my drawing table.
He's been up here drawing all night!


There was something about the whole process—the nuts and bolts—of making a comic...

Coming up with an idea.

daydreaming and drawing

Designing characters.

Figuring out the story, changing it around.

In the next panel she can say "Not yet."

Drawing the art in pencil first.

Lettering the words.

Inking the art.

It latched onto something in my brain and I fed off it.

COMICS

It was stimulating and engaging in a way that nothing else was for me at the time.

FREE FALLIN

GLUGLUGLUG

More!
CLUNK
DEW

Gosh—I could almost make a sculpture out of these!

I wouldn't go down there...
They're fighting again.

It's my **goddamn** money!

Maybe if I just wait a little...

CRASH
I worked hard for that money! It's mine, and I can spend it how I want!
So you can buy a-a **race car?!**

A race car?!

I've been saving this money for **years** from my extra freelance work!
And you never told me?!

Don't you think it might help with some of our bills?!
With the property taxes?
Or for the kids' college?!
Why do they always do this?

SLAM STOMP
SMASH
It's extra money I worked my butt off for—it's mine!
I'm **sick** of this!

I'm tired of putting up with this!

ENOUGH

STOP IT! STOP IT NOW!
I realized something...
I'm bigger than him now...
I'm not afraid anymore!
I'm sick of this crap! I'm not putting up with it ever again!

You wonder why I'm always over at a friend's?
Or shut in my room?!
THIS
This is why!

You're not allowed to do this anymore! You're acting like a spoiled baby!
You're a bully, and I've had enough of it.

I don't have to listen to this!
I had vowed to never lose my temper again, but something suddenly snapped in me. All the anger and frustration and resentment that had built up over the years just—

Don't you walk away from me!
Listen to me! Stop it!
STOP IT RIGHT NOW!
LEAP
AH!
STOP IT!
STOP IT!
THUMP
THUMP
AUGH
Oh my God, no—don't do this!

What's going on?!

SOB
SEEEEEETHE

SOB

I still managed to have moments with my family...

...but for the most part, I wanted to be somewhere else, with someone else.

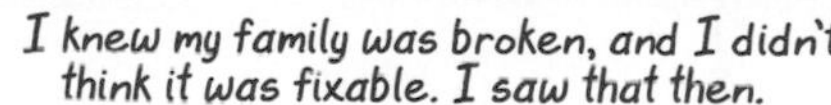

And my friends were...well, my friends.
You wanna do something after school?
Sure.

Maybe they teased me sometimes, but...
Why don't I come over?
Naw, I'll come over to your house.

It was nothing compared to the drama and tension at home.

So of course I was going to spend more time at my friends'.
How come you never want to hang at your house?

I didn't have any other options.
Because...you've got *Monkey Island 2* at your house!
Good point! I'll call you when I'm done with my homework.

But one day I'll meet that one special person.
Someone who will be a friend **and** care about me.

I really wish I could just have a girlfriend...

Someone to spend my life with.
To be my partner.
Then everything would be perfect.

Can you make me not fat and let me have a girlfriend?

What if the Ritalin is making me fat?

AIN'T NOTHIN' BUT A HOUND DOG
ROCKIN ALL TH
YOU AIN'T
Hi!
VRRRRMMM

How was school?
NEVE
AUGHT A RABBIT AND YOU AIN'T NO FRE
Fine, I guess.

Hmm—I'm pretty sure Mom's drug reference book is—AH!
VRRR

Let's see...
Ritalin... Methylphenidate...
Huh.
NURSE'S DRUG REFERENCE

**Loss** of appetite?! Weight **loss**?!
METHYLPHENIDATE
I need a cookie...

Mom's drug book said Ritalin makes people **lose** weight...
BATMAN
...but what if it's doing something else to me?

Do I even need to keep taking it? I'm in tenth grade and doing fine in school...Maybe I can try going off it over the summer...

So one day after summer break was well underway...
YAWN
BA
...I woke up and didn't take my pill.

The world didn't end.
RITALIN

I guess my ADHD is all gone!

Just at the time I was "done" with ADHD, it seemed to suddenly be everywhere.

EXTRA
EXTRA
EVERYONE HAS ADHD

BUT

Physicians and scientists have been writing about such behavior for a long time.

OMG

It's just the terms **ATTENTION DEFICIT DISORDER** or **ATTENTION DEFICIT HYPERACTIVITY DISORDER** that are relatively new.

**1775** Melchior Adam Weikard writes a medical textbook with a chapter on attention issues.

Personal doctor to Russian Empress Catherine II

**1798** Sir Alexander Crichton writes about "Mental Restlessness."

He describes kids who "have the fidgets" and who are "incapable of attending with constancy to any one object of education. Every impression seems to agitate the person. These children need special educational intervention."

**1845** "Fidgety Philip" poem about a kid who can't sit still at dinner.

Sit ye down at yon table!

**1902** Sir George F. Still gives a prominent lecture at the Royal College of Physicians in London.

"These kids are often aggressive, defiant, resistent to discipline, excessively emotional or passionate, show little inhibitory volition, and cannot learn from the consequences of their actions."

He posits some degree of biological basis.

**1932** Drs. Franz Kramer and Hans Pollnow write about a "Hyperkinetic Disease of Infancy" where kids demonstrate "marked restlessness" and more.

The kids they studied:

- Ran up and down the room
- Couldn't sit still
- Would climb about on furniture
- Would touch or move everything around them without pursuing a goal
- Were unable to concentrate on different tasks
- Failed to finish chores or work
- Displayed excessive motor activity with a conspicuous lack of purposefulness.

As the study of mental health developed in the twentieth century, doctors and scientists found it helpful to label and categorize the behaviors they were seeing.
Let's see... You'll be Sneezy, Dopey, and Bashful.
DOH

It was initially thought kids who couldn't pay attention and were hyper had some form of minor brain damage.
Well, he's got a steel bar through his head—no wonder he can't concentrate.

1957 Minimal brain damage

| 1963 | 1968 | 1980 | 1987 |
| --- | --- | --- | --- |
| It's decided you can't infer brain damage from bad behavior. | Doctor's observations are classified as an official diagnosis and encoded in the first update of the Diagnostic and Statistical Manual. | The name and details of the diagnosis are updated in DSM-III to focus on attentional issues. | DSM III-R adds "hyperactivity" to the name of the diagnosis. |
| Minimal brain dysfunction | Hyperkinetic Reaction of Childhood | Attention Deficit Disorder | Attention Deficit Hyperactivity Disorder |

The Diagnostic and Statistical Manual (DSM) contains the official names and descriptions of mental health disorders. The first edition was in 1952.

So prior to 1980, the terms "ADD" or "ADHD" did not exist, but the behaviors certainly did. It is our understanding and labeling of those behaviors that have changed.

It is one part medical science...
We've discovered several genes we think might contribute to ADHD behaviors.
Cool!

...and one part social science.
You go over there. You're being disruptive!
DISRUPTIVE

Just as ADHD didn't come out of nowhere, it also wasn't "invented" by drug companies to sell pills to kids.

(A common claim from those who think ADHD is fake.)

In fact, almost all psychiatric meds have been discovered by accident.

RITALIN was first made in 1944 by Leandro Panizzon, who named the drug after his wife, nicknamed "Rita."

It helps with my low blood pressure!

But it wasn't identified as a stimulant until the 1950s as pharmaceutal companies raced to find "silver bullets" for mental health treatments.

YES, pharmaceutical companies want to sell as many pills as possible because they're in business to make money, and they can often go too far in their quest for "product awareness," often done under the guise of "**EDUCATIONAL MATERIAL.**"

This has certainly led to some people being wrongly diagnosed and medicated but also to an increase in people who need treatment getting help.

Sure, you can give this to a three-year-old!

This story we definitely didn't pay for and write says it's safe!
TAKE IT

This pamphlet we definitely didn't write and pay for encourages you to evaluate ALL your students.
SCHO

Here's a sample. This one's free!

BUT THE REALITY IS

medication works. About 80% of ADHDers respond to stimulant meds with a positive effect on symptoms.

There is no other medication for a psychiatric condition with such a high rate of effectiveness.

I can focus at school. I can get things done and learn to control myself.

Though medication isn't the ONLY treatment option nor should it be the first!

It's understandable why ADHD is hard for people to grasp.

It's not a discrete disease like the chicken pox or flu.

# ADHD IS REAL.

Just as real as clinical depression. They're even diagnosed in very similar ways—via clinical symptoms, questionnaires, observation, rating scales, etc.

But in the same way that being very sad sometimes doesn't mean you're depressed...

...being forgetful or distracted or hyper from time to time doesn't mean you have ADHD...

...or that it's not a real thing.

ADHD has its roots in fundamental differences in genetics and brain structure. It's part of who you are as a person.

And while you can treat it, you can't escape it.

I started eleventh grade that fall without meds for the first time in eight years.
HIGH SCHOOL

Everything seemed the same after I went off my meds. At least I thought so.

With hindsight, I saw—slowly but surely—I became more social, more wacky, less reserved. More like I was in private.
You're so sarcastic this year!
CHEMISTRY

I was coming out of my shell. Who was this kid? Where did he come from?
RAR
AH! GODZILLA!

At the time I thought...
I've known most of these people for ten or eleven years. I feel comfortable around them and am finally letting myself relax.
You goof!
YUCK YUCK

But something more was going on. My body was changing, too, and it wasn't just puberty.

I'd been taking Ritalin in one form or another every day for the last eight years, and now suddenly it wasn't there in my body.

CIBA

(I hadn't talked to my doctor before stopping my meds. While I didn't notice any negative side effects, I now know I should have talked to him before making that change.)

Over the course of about eighteen months, I grew—**up**ward instead of outward for once.

JUNE 1993
SEPT 1994

I shot up several inches and seventy pounds melted from my body.

Mom—I need new pants!

I spent eleventh grade going through this physical and social metamorphosis that, in retrospect, was brought on by the absence of the Ritalin.

RADIO K
MATH

At home, I'd always been a silly, gregarious person and now more of that personality came out in public.

Puppet show of Ibsen's "Master Builder."
HA HA
HA HA
HA HA
HA HA
HA

And while I felt the realistic possibility of having a girlfriend for the first time, I was still in many ways too immature to deal with that.

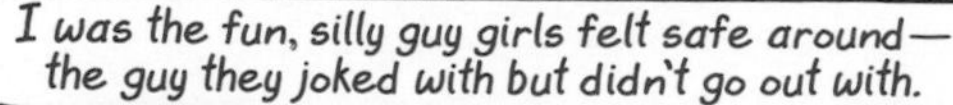

Most important, from my parents' perspective, I was doing "well."

My grades were good, and I had a growing circle of friends and activities.

And I hadn't gotten involved in anything harmful or dangerous, been arrested, or crashed the car.*

*All things ADHDers do at a higher rate.

I was focused on things I cared about and found interesting. That came through to others around me.

And then, as graduation and the pull of leaving home grew near, I had an idea...

My dad grew up in Indianapolis, so the race was a really big part of his life.

And by extension, it was a part of my life growing up, too.

I'd been to the track before many times while visiting my grandparents, but never on race day.

So there was some selfish interest, but it also felt like...

...this was one last thing I could share with my dad. One last "nice" memory I could make with him before moving out and basically saying "goodbye" to my family.

It was a long and uncomfortable drive.
Z
Neck sore from sleeping in car

And my dad was...my dad.
#@?$!

I mostly pretended it wasn't happening and focused on the positive stuff.
MMM! This is a really good burger!

We had fun and enjoyed the race.

And part of me felt at peace with my dad.
Z

It would be many years before my mom found any peace...
RAWR
SMASH

...when my parents finally divorced.
I want a divorce.

It happened long after I stopped thinking it could.
I'm not completely surprised. I can't believe it didn't happen sooner.
MALT SHOP
I think it will be better for everyone.

My mom and brother moved back to Indiana to be with her family.
We found a cute little house in town, right down the road from the farm.
It even has an extra room I can use for an art studio!
Neat! I'll come visit once you're settled in.
DISH

I came home from the Indy 500 and partied with my friends.
WHS

Graduated high school with honors.

And spent time with my friends before we all headed off to the next chapters of our lives.

Are you going to be ready?
Yeah, I've just got a few more things.
ZZTOP

There were so many questions that **could** have been lingering in my head then.
TY college


About my future, my family, me.

Will I become like my dad?
What if I have kids?
WUMP
Am I too much of a weirdo to ever get married?

But right then, I wasn't thinking about those questions. I was happy and excited about the future, on my own.

ADHD wasn't something I really thought about anymore.

My doctor and parents never used the term "ADD" or "ADHD" but they did say:

YOU'LL GROW OUT OF IT.

And that's what I thought had happened.

Accepted wisdom at the time said ADHD was a disorder of young boys and they'd "grow out of it" as they matured.

But we know differently now.

ABOUT 2/3

of kids diagnosed with ADHD will continue to struggle with symptoms as an adult.

It affects people of all ages, ethnicities, and genders.

And a growing number of people are being diagnosed for the first time as adults, after a lifetime of frustrations.

These are often people (usually girls) who aren't physically hyper. They may be high functioning enough to still get good grades and avoid obvious trouble, so they slide under the diagnostic radar.

Until they smack into the challenges of adult life.

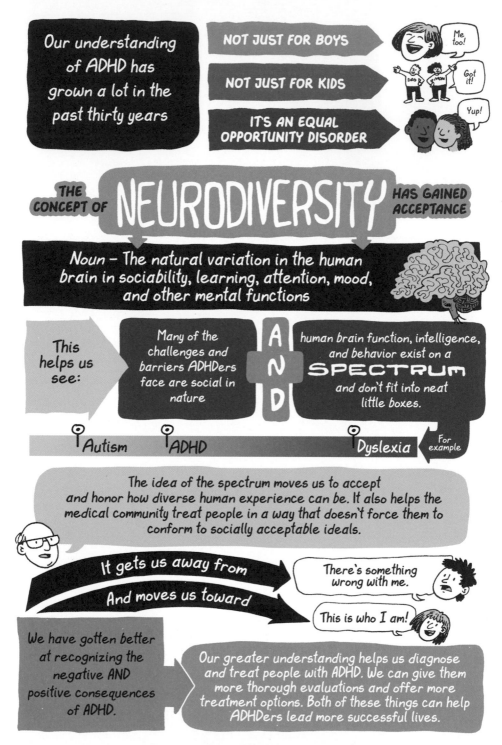

Our understanding of ADHD has grown a lot in the past thirty years

NOT JUST FOR BOYS

NOT JUST FOR KIDS

IT'S AN EQUAL OPPORTUNITY DISORDER

Yup!

THE CONCEPT OF **NEURODIVERSITY** HAS GAINED ACCEPTANCE

*Noun* – The natural variation in the human brain in sociability, learning, attention, mood, and other mental functions

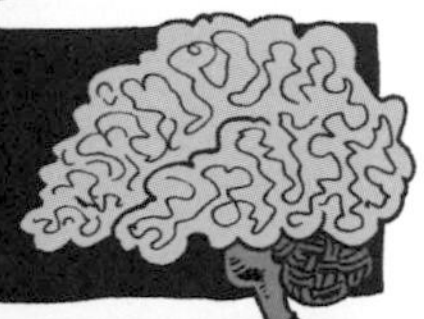

This helps us see:

Many of the challenges and barriers ADHDers face are social in nature

AND

human brain function, intelligence, and behavior exist on a SPECTRUM and don't fit into neat little boxes.

For example

Autism — ADHD — Dyslexia

The idea of the spectrum moves us to accept and honor how diverse human experience can be. It also helps the medical community treat people in a way that doesn't force them to conform to socially acceptable ideals.

It gets us away from

There's something wrong with me.

And moves us toward

This is who I am!

We have gotten better at recognizing the negative AND positive consequences of ADHD.

Our greater understanding helps us diagnose and treat people with ADHD. We can give them more thorough evaluations and offer more treatment options. Both of these things can help ADHDers lead more successful lives.

For example—we now understand how ADHD presents itself changes over time.

Adult ADHD often looks very different than childhood ADHD and is often different for men and women.

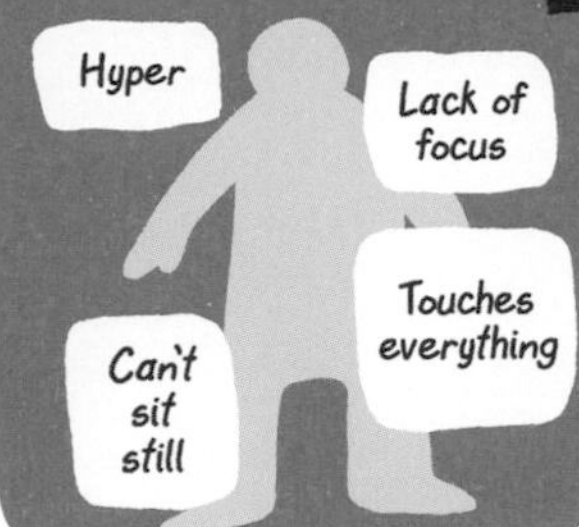


The external symptoms of children

Lack of focus
Touches everything

tend to become more internalized as people age.

• Restlessness
• Racing thoughts
• Anxiety
• Disorganization
• Risk-prone tendencies
• etc.

An adult with ADHD may appear normal but on the inside...

So on page thirty-five of the report, you'll see...

DIDN'T GET

THAT'S

OMG what's happening?

LEAVE ME?

TAP YOUR LEG

TAP TAP TAP

We develop coping strategies as we age to meet social norms.

As an adult, these symptoms can lead to an entirely different set of problems unique to the adult world:
Substance abuse
Financial trouble
Legal problems
Health problems
Employment issues
Family and social problems


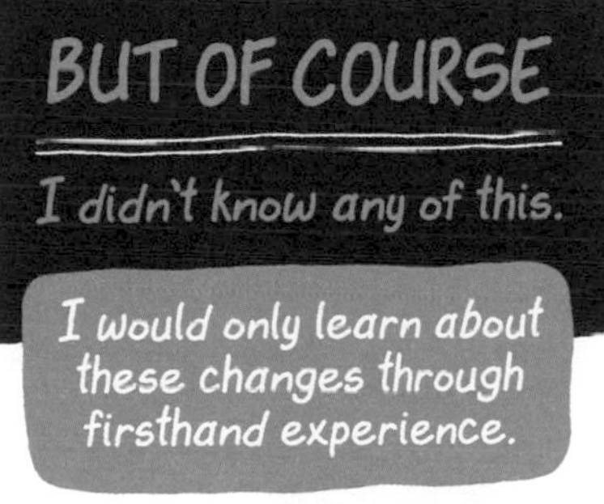

BUT OF COURSE
I didn't know any of this.
I would only learn about these changes through firsthand experience.

Adulthood

I would think about ADHD again someday.
Bye.
WHEATIES
TOUR
RABBIT

My greatest life challenges related to ADHD were actually ahead of me.
ZZTOP
Drive safe!

Relationships, work...
...marriage...
...parenting.

But
that's another
story.

# AUTHOR'S NOTE

Communicating what it's like to live with ADHD is tricky because everyone feels distracted, unfocused, forgetful, out of control, or hyperactive from time to time. ADHD is a disorder of degrees; those of us with ADHD have those feelings more often than other people, and, to a degree, that becomes troublesome for us. It impacts our school, social, and family lives.

It is also tricky because ADHD is a life-span issue. It's not something that just comes up once, or for a year or two, and is gone. *Button Pusher* is an amalgamation of things that happened to me over the course of eight years. I was diagnosed when I was eight years old and went off meds when I was sixteen. I could have written an entire book about nothing but the ways I misbehaved, was out of control, got in trouble, or was emotionally immature, but that wouldn't have made for a very good book.

So for the purposes of telling a coherent (and entertaining!) narrative, I streamlined a lot of events and tried my best to highlight key moments when ADHD impacted my schooling, my friendships, and my family. I (hopefully) showcased the times in my childhood that best illustrated the difficulties and challenges that come with ADHD.

Is this exactly how things happened? For the most part. Anyone who has launched into a story about their lives knows they make choices about how to tell that story—which details to include or leave out, and so forth. This was my best attempt at recalling what it was like growing up with ADHD. If there were places where I couldn't remember something exactly, I focused on making sure that the emotions I felt at the time came through. I have mashed together people, places, and events, and played around a little with the timeline. In the end, it all rings true and should hopefully help you understand how tricky ADHD can be.

My hope is that this book helps fellow ADHDers feel a little less alone and better understood and that it helps parents and other caregivers understand what this is like for a child.

The medical and scientific information provided is pulled from research I did for my book *Raised on Ritalin*. A full bibliography can be found in that book or on my website stylishvittles.com for those interested.

## Tyler, Age 8

3rd Grade, Armatage Elementary, right before being diagnosed with ADD

**Enjoys:**

Drawing,
riding his bike,
playing with Legos,
plain cheese pizza

**Dislikes:**

Eggs

## Tyler, Age 43

Family camping trip, Gooseberry Falls State Park, Minnesota

**Enjoys:**

Drawing,
riding his bike,
playing Legos with his kids,
pepperoni pizza

**Dislikes:**

Eggs

# THANK YOU!

Thank you to:
My agent, Britt Siess, who was there to answer the call when I decided to try "one more time." Without her insistence, this book might not have happened.

My editors, Calista and Alex, who understood the complexity of this story and topic and helped make it even better.

The rest of the First Second team who helped make this book look amazing.

Joe Flood for his coloring assistance. This book wouldn't look quite as good without his extra help and hard work.

My friends who read early drafts and offered feedback, and who have supported my work over the years.

The doctors, clinicians, and researchers whose work I spent years poring over, and the librarians and colleagues who helped me find it.

The Graphic Medicine community who embraced me and my work and showed me there was other work out there like this.

My coworkers and my intrepid staff at MCAD who allowed me the flexibility to work on this project.

And to my family: the one I grew up with, and the one I've made for myself. Your love and support have made all the difference. Thanks for believing in me.

Special shout-out to my kids: This book would not exist without you!

# CHILDHOOD ART

Drawing has been a part of my entire life. I've been making comics in some form or another since elementary school.

My own version of a Garfield strip with our family cat as the star.

Indestructible robot designing phase.

In junior high, I started to get more serious about making comics.

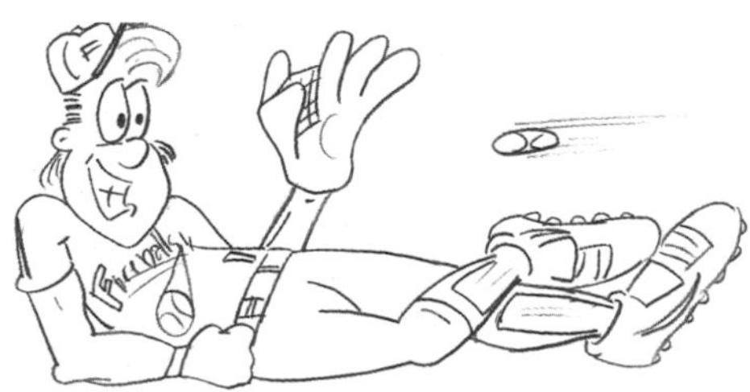

In middle school, I made up a whole baseball team and did strips about them for my friends and classmates.

# PROCESS

Most projects begin in my sketchbook. I jot down ideas and thoughts or draw images that pop into my head. It's kind of like brainstorming on paper.

Once I've got a lot of ideas that are working, I'll write a rough outline to organize them. This is just "This happens, then this happens," etc. I try to do one paragraph per scene. That way I can move it around or rearrange it if it's decided that scene works better in a different part of the book.

INFO #5
Labels - what are they good for?

Jon and Tyler at bus stop.
~~A new family has moved into the neighborhood and they come to introduce themselves to Tyler's family. There is a boy, Jon, who is Tyler's age and they start hanging out.~~ But Jon introduces a new element to Tyler's friend group. One day at the bus stop Jon teases Tyler for being too fat to catch them in a game of tag. Tyler is enraged by this and tries to catch Jon. Tyler never catches him and accidentally steps on his backpack, causing his lunch to explode. Tyler is furious when he gets on the bus, but during the bus ride his anger vanishes. Tyler thinks about this, how it's like he has "emotional amnesia" but also that his temper is like his Dad - it's like a switch flipping on or off in his brain.

INFO #6
Emotional regulation

This is the initial outline for the scene with Jon at the bus stop, that starts on page 169.

Next I use the outline to write a rough script. I try to break it down into pages and panels. It's pretty sparse, as I like to leave much of the creative decisions to the drawing phase, but I'll include important notes when needed (like a character's clothing, or they're moving in a certain direction, etc.).

PG167-168
LABELS - what's in a label? Good/bad?
The label didn't mean much to me because it was never used but I would start hearing it more often

PG169- BUS SCENE
1) As school starts up again Jon was no longer 'the new kid.' He was just one of the gang.

2) But he wasn't always on my side.
But as he got more comfortable in his new home, he became more disruptive.
Playing tag at the bus stop. Someone tags not Tyler- you're it!

3) Tyler and friends run.

4) Tyler ducks a tag

5) Tyler is swatted- TAG

PG170
1) Kids run away from Tyler- he'll never catch us!

I did a full rough draft for *Button Pusher*. These were just bare-bones drawings to work out the page layout and character and text placement, and to check that the story flowed well. (Also to sketch karate rats or whatever else I was thinking about.)

For inking, I scan in my penciled pages and print them out on 9x12 Bristol in a special light blue color that the scanner won't pick up. I used a variety of Micron pens. They provided the line quality I wanted for this book, and they're easier to carry around than a kit of brushes and ink bottles.

Next is penciling on plain computer paper. Working smaller helps me work faster and keep things from becoming too precious.

Then the inked pages are scanned and cleaned up. Coloring is done in Photoshop, and lettering is done in InDesign using a font I designed based on some of my own hand lettering.

The medical information in this book is provided as an informational resource only and should not be used or relied upon for any diagnostic or treatment purposes. This information does not create any patient-physician relationship and should not be used as a substitute for professional diagnosis and treatment.

The names and identifying characteristics of some persons described in this book have been changed, as have dates, places, and other details of events depicted in the book.

First Second

Published by First Second
First Second is an imprint of Roaring Brook Press,
a division of Holtzbrinck Publishing Holdings Limited Partnership
120 Broadway, New York, NY 10271
firstsecondbooks.com
mackids.com



Library of Congress Control Number: 2021913188

First edition, 2022
Edited by Calista Brill and Alex Lu
Cover design by Kirk Benshoff
Interior book design by Molly Johanson
Color assistance by Joe Flood

Penciled with a mechanical pencil on copy paper. Scanned into Photoshop, converted to non-photo blue, and printed on 9x12 Bristol paper. Inked with various-size Micron pens. Colored digitally in Photoshop.

Printed in March 2022 in China by 1010 Printing International Limited, Kwun Tong, Hong Kong

ISBN 978-1-250-75833-0 (paperback)
3 5 7 9 10 8 6 4

ISBN 978-1-250-75834-7 (hardcover)
3 5 7 9 10 8 6 4 2